Family Walks around Birmingham & West Midlands

HIGH INTEREST · LOW MILEAGE

Scarthin Books of Cromford
Derbyshire
1996

Family Walks Series

THE COUNTRY CODE

Guard against all risk of fire
Fasten all gates
Keep dogs under proper control
Keep to paths across farmland
Avoid damaging fences, hedges and walls
Leave no litter
Safeguard water supplies
Protect wildlife, plants and trees
Go carefully on country roads
Respect the life of the countryside

Published by Scarthin Books, Cromford, Derbyshire, 1996

Phototypesetting by Paragon Typesetters, Newton-le-Willows, Merseyside

Printed by Redwood Books

Walks 6, 7, 8, 9, 11, 12, 13, 14, 15, 16, 17, 18 © Geoff Allen, 1993
(previously published in ''Family Walks in Warwickshire'')

Walks 1, 2, 3, 4, 5, 27, 28, 29, 30 © Les Lumsdon and Chris Rushton, 1995

Walks 21, 22, 25, 26 © Gordon Ottewell, 1988
(previously published in ''Family Walks in Hereford and Worcester''

Walk 19 © Gordon Ottewell, 1992
(previously published in ''Family Walks around Stratford and Banbury'')

Walks 10, 20, 23, 24, 31, 32 © John Roberts, 1995

Edited by Guy Cooper

Maps by Ivan Sendall

Photographs by the authors

Cover photograph: Warwick Castle and River. Courtesy Birmingham Picture Library

ISBN 0 907758 83 5

Kenilworth Castle (Route 15)

ABOUT THE AUTHORS

Geoff Allen is an early-retired insurance official turned journalist, with over 35 years of regular walking behind him. His rambles have been appearing weekly in the *Birmingham Evening Mail* since 1980 and he has long been the Midlands reporter of *The Great Outdoors* magazine. He is the secretary of his local rambling club and is the author of *Family Walks in Warwickshire*, from which many walks in this book are taken.

Les Lumsdon is a Senior Lecturer in Tourism at Staffordshire Polytechnic. He is married with three children and lives in Macclesfield. He has written several other books on walking, including *Family Walks in Staffordshire Peak & Potteries* and (with David Gorvett) *Black & White Village Trail*.

Gordon Ottewell was a colliery surveyor in his native Derbyshire before becoming a teacher. He was Primary Head in Oxfordshire and Gloucestershire until his retirement. Countryside exploration has been his lifelong passion and he leads walking tours of the Cotswolds, where he now lives. He is a regular contributor to *Cotswold Life* and *Gloucestershire Echo* and is the author of a number of walking books, including six in the *Family Walks* series.

John Roberts grew up in the Wirral and all but two of his eight homes have been on the edges of towns so walking and the landscape have always been part of his life. He worked in Insurance and became a lecturer in insurance and law. He started writing and publishing walks in his spare time and, after some years developing the *Walkways* imprint, turned to full time publishing and writing.

Contents

Map of the Area

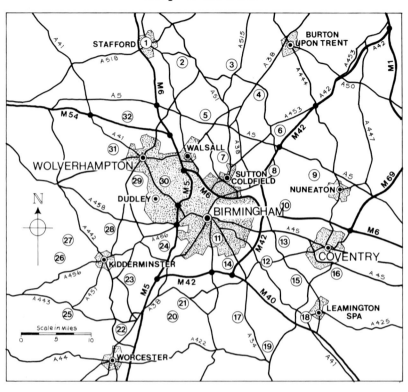

INTRODUCTION

People who live in the West Midlands are incredibly lucky. All round one of the biggest, densest areas of industry and housing in the world is glorious countryside. And it is covered by hundreds of miles of footpaths, tracks and quiet lanes which make it one of the best walking areas in Britain.

To the north is the high, gravelly heathland of Cannock Chase, with birch and bilberry, bracken and pines rising over steep little hills. In the east, the folded green of Warwickshire rises from the watery bottom of the Tame Valley to the hills that tower over Nuneaton. In the south-east is the Arden country, woods and farms and pretty villages. All round the southern edge of the conurbation is that exciting range of hills from the Lickeys to Kinver Edge, and beyond it a distant rural plain which falls gently into the valleys of the Rivers Severn and Avon. To the west is the most fascinating country of all, nobly rounded hills, woodland and pasture, with the Severn Valley and Wyre Forest. Many people feel that this area is scenically equal to the Cotswolds, or better, and much less arable and populated.

Choosing a walk
The walks in this book have all been selected with children in mind. None is especially steep or difficult and your best guide to a walk to suit you and your kids is probably the distance. There is mud, but they may like that. Allow plenty of time, take frequent rests and have a good break in the middle. You might think in terms of an average of one mile or two miles per hour, depending on their age, and, of course, your own.

Refreshments
We have noted suitable pubs and cafes, but not all walks have them. Carry some food, and especially drinks. Experiments have shown that walkers given regular liquid do not feel as tired as those who take bigger drinks at longer intervals. I would guess that this is more true of children. Regular drinks are not a fun extra, they are essential.

Finding the way
We sincerely hope that with our route directions and maps you should have no trouble at all. You should not need any further maps for the walks, but you will find the Ordnance Survey Landranger Sheets useful for finding starting points. They are also sufficiently detailed to be helpful en route if you are in any doubt.

By far the most likely cause of doubt which might make the directions puzzling is that something out there has changed. Hedges do vanish, ponds dry up or are created, houses are built and stiles and gates come and go. If you find the scene not entirely as the directions suggest, this is probably the reason.

What to wear
These walks are not mountaineering expeditions. Go in whatever ordinary clothes seem comfortable, but consider these points.
1. Most people seem to prefer walking boots, but I find trainers excellent in dryer

weather. Wear wellies if you like; many people find them hot and sweaty for a walk of more than a couple of miles. Socks are most important, as thick and woolly as possible, and it is worth looking for those with loop pile.

2. You may at times be glad of a hat, a waterproof, gloves and spare sweater. The risible woollen bobble hat actually does its job very well, but you can get more sophisticated jobs.

3. Denim is heavy and absorbs water without releasing it. Jeans of any material may be cut too close around the hips and legs for walking. You could look for polyester/cotton trousers, or try corduroy in winter.

4. Consider the advantages of garments that open all down the front such as outdoor shirts and cardigans. In cold weather you can button up, but open by cautious degrees for ventilation. In summer you can wear a brushed cotton shirt open or closed to any degree, in our out of your trousers, and with sleeves rolled up or down.

These walks explore all of this country, from Cannock Chase to Hanbury in Worcestershire, from Hartshill Hayes near Atherstone to the Wyre Forest. They come from four well known writers of walks in the Midlands with tens of thousands of miles and years of experience to share with you. Come with us and celebrate your countryside.

John Roberts
1996

Map Key

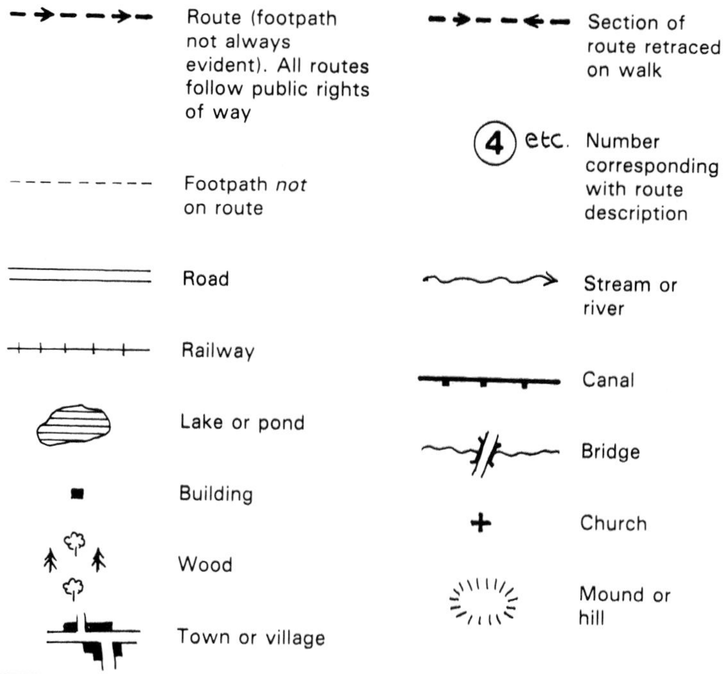

- ▶ - - ▶ -   Route (footpath not always evident). All routes follow public rights of way

- - - - - - - -   Footpath *not* on route

═══════   Road

+ + + + +   Railway

Lake or pond

■   Building

Wood

Town or village

- ▶ - - ◀ -   Section of route retraced on walk

④ etc.   Number corresponding with route description

Stream or river

━━━━   Canal

Bridge

✚   Church

Mound or hill

Stafford High House

Stafford

Outline
Stafford Railway Station − Stafford Castle − Derrington − Burleyfields − Stafford Railway Station

Summary
A walk which begins through new housing but soon climbs up to the majestic remains of Stafford Castle. The route then follows paths and bridleways across fields to Derrington, including a dank underpass beneath the M6 motorway. The return section is along the Stafford to Newport Greenway.

Attractions
Stafford Castle stands on a site which has been fortified since the 12th century. The castle was improved throughout the medieval period. The keep was reconstructed in the 19th century in the Gothic Revival style. Up until the 1950s the castle lay in ruins and in 1961 was given to Stafford Borough. It has since been the subject of much restoration and is open to the public.

Stafford itself is a joy to walk around and in the centre is the Ancient High House where the Tourist Information Centre is situated along with displays and exhibitions. Some might wish to pick up leaflets explaining other local walks, including one to Doxey Marshes which is an ideal short walk from the town. The Marshes are wetlands which attract a variety of birdlife. Part of the Marshes is a Site of Special Scientific Interest.

Refreshments
There are plenty of cafes and inns in Stafford, including the Stafford Arms Hotel near to the station.

Public Transport
Stafford Railway Station is well served by trains from the West Midlands daily. It is also the terminus for long distance bus services from Lichfield and Tamworth.

Route 1

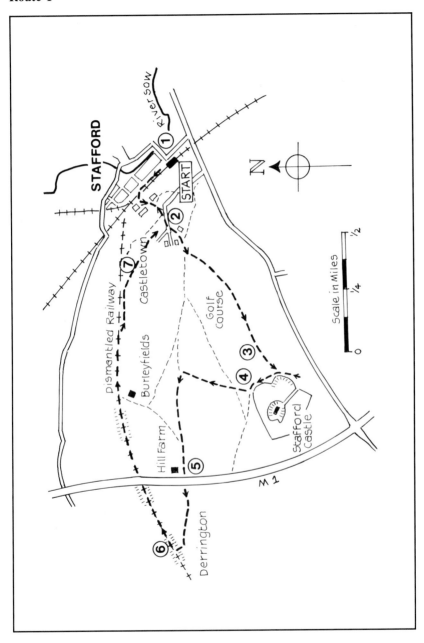

Route 1

Stafford

4 miles

Start

Stafford Railway Station (OS Landranger Sheet 127, GR 918229).

Route

1. *Turn left from the station to walk along Station Road past the Stafford Arms Hotel. Follow the road as it bends left to continue alongside the railway. It curves up to another junction by the Railway Arms. Go left here to cross a bridge over the railway.*

2. *You reach a kissing gate. Cross a road with a large roundabout to the left. A little link path runs ahead to the next road. Cross this and then follow the path as it bends left by houses and alongside a hedge. The well worn route runs up the hillside with a golf course to your left.*

3. *This eventually comes to a stile which gives out into a field before the castle grounds. If you are going to visit the castle go ahead to another stile and then to a track and castle entrance on the right.*

4. *Otherwise go slightly right across a field. Cross a stile and bear right down the field's edge. You follow this until you reach a wood, but, just before, go left to walk ahead to a bridle gate. Then continue ahead towards Stallbrook Hall, but as you near it do not go on to the road. Instead stay in the field and bear slightly left to another bridlegate.*

5. *Once through cut down to walk beneath the motorway in eerie silence only to re-emerge to the constant hum of noise once again. Walk ahead along a line of oaks, then head in the direction of the houses at Derrington as signposted slightly right. Cross a stile and a gate beneath the hawthorns and make your way through to the lane.*

6. *Go right and walk ahead to the underbridge. Just before, go left up the embankment to the old track bed. Turn right and ramble back towards Stafford, passing by Burleyfields Farm on the right. Leave the old track to join the lane on the right and turn left along it.*

7. *This runs back into a new housing estate. Keep ahead to the point where you crossed this road on the outward section. Go left through a kissing gate and return to Stafford Railway Station.*

Milford

14

Milford Common, Cannock Chase

Outline

Milford Common − Oat Hill − Stepping Stones − Marquis's Drive − Stepping Stones − Brocton Coppice − Milford Common

Summary

Cannock Chase is one of Staffordshire's favourite places for walking. The paths are clear on the ground, but do take care at junctions for there is a maze of tracks, some of which are for forestry access only. There are several climbs on this walk, which features heathland, coniferous and deciduous woodland. It is a great place for picnics too.

Attractions

Cannock Chase is an ideal destination for children at all times of the year. In summer, they will run to the streams and pools. In the winter they love to wrap dreams around the intricate silver cobwebs dangling from the trees and to search for the elusive fallow deer hidden amongst bush and bracken.

The Chase would have been covered completely by deciduous woodland in previous centuries, retained as a hunting preserve for local nobility. Then as shipbuilding and the smelting of charcoal became more developed vast expanses of this one time natural forest were hacked down for short term commercial gain rather like the way in which major forests are being felled in other parts of the world today. It is interesting to note how history repeats itself, but hopefully we have learned some lessons from our predecessors.

Shugborough Hall, the 18th century ancestral home of the Anson family and now lived in by the fifth earl, Patrick Lichfield, is a great place for a family visit. The Georgian mansion is something of an inspiration, as are the parklands where dramatic follies are to be found. Many families head for Shugborough Park Farm, especially on days when the farm is re-creating past events such as harvesting, smocking or working with shire horses. There's also a restored corn mill driven by a water wheel.

A walk on the Chase and a visit to nearby Shugborough (the entrance is by Milford Common) make for an excellent day out whatever the season.

Refreshments

There are cafes at the Common and pubs nearby.

Public Transport

Milford Common is served by buses from Stafford, Cannock and Lichfield.

Route 2

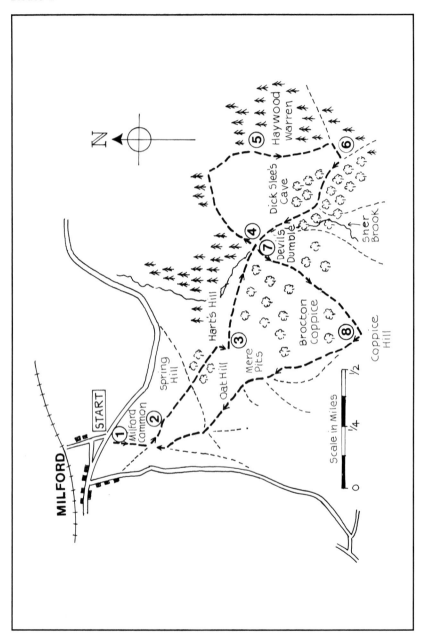

Route 2

Milford Common, Cannock Chase   5 miles

Start
Milford Common car park (OS Landranger Sheet 127, GR 973211).

Route
1. *With your back to the Information Board walk up steps, on The Heart of England Way, a long distance footpath through the Midlands, and then ahead a short distance until the path forks. Keep ahead and descend steps into a trough. Bear right and walk up the valley, with bracken to the right and trees to the left. This leads to another path at a junction before a pond.*

2. *Bear second left up a main path leading up the hillside between picnic tables. The path then dips down to pass another pool known as Long Mere on the right, and just beyond its edge curves to the right to climb once again. At the top the path bends gently right and comes to a junction on level ground. Take the path bearing very slightly left down the wooded hillside which soon drops to a main path by a gate.*

3. *Turn right and at the next junction turn left to proceed along the Staffordshire Way through the woodland into the Sherbrook Valley. You will soon reach the stepping stones across the Sher Brook. There are also picnic tables here.*

4. *Once across the water you climb out of the valley. After a quarter of a mile the wide path levels and you need to look for a steeper path rising up to the right in a clearing. There is no real landmark, simply a No Horse Riding sign.*

5. *Pass a square enclosure and proceed ahead to reach a much larger open area. At the marker post HH3 bear right and at the top of the green go left. You will come to a junction where you go right and then left at marker HH1. Dick Slee's cave, a small cave once said to be a hiding place for scoundrels, is near here.*

6. *You soon meet a track which descends the bank. At the crossroads below go right along Marquis's Drive. This drops gradually between bracken into the Sherbrook valley. Ignore turnings to the left but keep ahead. You emerge on to the track by the stepping stones. Go left and cross them.*

7. *At the crossroads go ahead to climb the opposite bank up to Brocton Coppice. You eventually rise up to a major junction where you follow the blue waymarker right and right again. The track curves right and then falls away towards the valley once more. It then bends left to join another track. Go next right and walk above a pool to your left at Mere Pits.*

8. *You come to a crossroads. Your way is to the left down a long incised incline to a junction of paths below. Bear right here as signposted, but within a few paces head along the main path which curves left and then right to pass Sister Dora's Home and then down in a slightly right direction back to the car park. It is gratifying to know that much of this 30,000 acre area of natural beauty is threaded with footpaths ideal for family walks.*

Hamstall Ridware

Outline
Hamstall Ridware — Nethertown — Pipe Ridware — Hunger Hill — Hamstall Ridware

Summary
The walk follows the flood plain of the Blithe valley through to Nethertown and Pipe Ridware. It then climbs a hillside to Hunger Hill, where there are good views across the Vale of Trent. At Hunger Hill you pass by a triangulation point which happens to be right in the middle of a field, such was the dedication of the Ordnance Survey to mapping.

Attractions
Ridware means the folk of the river. As the four villages and hamlets of the same name — Hamstall, Hill, Mavesyn and Pipe Ridware — lie between the flowing waters of the Blithe and Trent the name seems highly appropriate. Hamstall Ridware lies close to the Blithe, a pretty place with a church which is approached across a pasture and a handsome manor house nearby. The church contains several very old tombs, including the Cotton family where there are shields reflecting the family crests of 15 children of notable John Cotton.

Nearby Abbots Bromley attracts people from far and wide, for it is the home of the famous Horn Dance, an all day event which takes place on the first Monday after 4th September. Local stalwarts dress in costume and bear horns (which are kept in the church) when beating the bounds of the parish, covering as much as 20 miles. The 'horns' are thought to date from the 11th century. The butter market, roadside garage and village hostelries add to the picture of a very traditional Staffordshire village. The nearby Blithfield reservoir makes an ideal picnic spot.

Refreshments
The Shoulder of Mutton in Hamstall Ridware.

Public Transport
The Ridwares enjoy a limited bus service. Contact Staffordshire Bus on (01785) 223344 for details.

Route 3

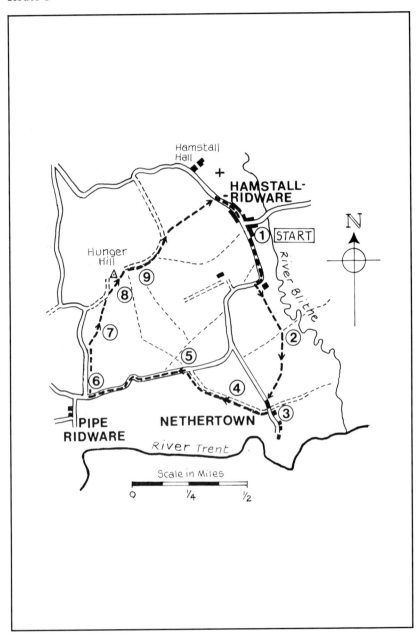

Route 3

Hamstall Ridware

3½ miles

Start

The Shoulder of Mutton, Hamstall Ridware (OS Landranger Sheet 128, GR 107189).

Route

1. *Turn left from the entrance to The Shoulder of Mutton and left again at the junction. At the edge of the village the road bends right. After a house you go left over a double stile. Follow the hedge on the left past barns belonging to the farm. Go through two gates and cross a stile by a hut. Then go left and right to follow the field's edge for a few metres.*

2. *However, now head slightly right across the field aiming for the far right and indented corner. Go through a gateway and bear slightly right over the next field to a stile by a gate. The buildings of Upper Netherton Farm stand to the right.*

3. *Join a road, go left and at a red brick dwelling known as Bancroft House in Nethertown, one of the quietest of hamlets in Staffordshire, go right. This track soon bends left by a dwelling. You keep ahead along a bridleway. This can get wet and the growth is thick in places.*

4. *It opens up to run alongside a field. The bridleway section is very overgrown and there's a ditch full of water, so it is best to follow the field's edge (marked on the map as a parallel path to the bridleway) to the field corner ahead.*

5. *Join the road and turn left to walk to a road junction just before the few houses of Pipe Ridware. To the left, across a field, you can see a little chapel converted into a theatre, which is well known locally for its productions.*

6. *Before the junction enter the field on your right by way of the large gates. Follow the hedge which actually runs parallel to the road on the left as it rises. Towards the top of the field cut right as waymarked to a stile in the next boundary which is awkward to climb.*

7. *Once across go right to cross another stile and then climb up the bluff to the left of the old scar and crescent of hawthorns. Go over a stile and proceed ahead over two others and through a pocket of woodland.*

8. *You should now be able to see the triangulation point in the middle of the field ahead, marking the summit of Hunger Hill. Aim just to the right of it and then*

21

towards a signpost to the left of a house. Cross the stile here and walk along the track, but for less than 100 metres.

9. *Go right over a stile after the entrance drive to a dwelling on the right. Once in the field turn left and keep company with the hedge to your left. At the corner go left and descend to the village, crossing another stile and then exiting on to the road in the village. The stile can be seen clearly to the right of houses. Turn right on the road and pass by the entrance to the church.*

Pipe Ridware Theatre

Fradley Junction

Route 4   **3 miles**

Fradley

Outline
Fradley School – The Sale – Fradley Junction – Fradley Bridge – Fradley

Summary
The walk runs through level fields which are usually under arable crops. You then walk a short road section to the Coventry Canal and join the towpath to Fradley Junction before returning to Fradley village.

Attractions
Fradley Junction is something of a mecca for waterways folk. It can get really busy at times as craft join the Trent and Mersey Canal from the Coventry Canal and vice versa. Fradley Junction is characterised by building and paraphernalia which date from the canal era and this makes it a most attractive place to visit.

Fradley itself is a small village which lies just off the busy A38 road. This follows the route of a major Roman thoroughfare, the Ryknild Way. North of Fradley is the pleasant town of Alrewas with its red brick houses and thatched cottages.

To the south is Lichfield, home to scribe Samuel Johnson and scientist Charles Darwin. The cathedral and its surroundings are magnificent and a walk at Fradley coupled with a detour to Lichfield makes for a good day out.

Refreshments
The Swan at Fradley Junction.

Public Transport
Fradley enjoys a limited bus service from Lichfield.

Route 4

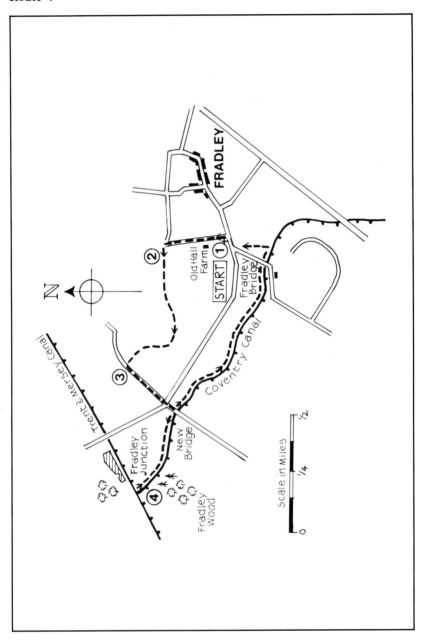

FRADLEY

Old Hall Farm

START ①

②

Fradley Bridge

Coventry Canal

N

Trent & Mersey Canal

③

Fradley Junction

New Bridge

④

Fradley Wood

Scale in Miles

0   ¼   ½

Route 4

Fradley   3 miles

Start

Fradley School in the village (OS Landranger Sheet 128, GR 157135).

Route

1. *From the school turn next left by Fradley Church to walk down Old Hall Lane. As the road bends right go ahead on a track, but within a few paces turn left to cross a stile into a field.*

2. *Keep company with a hedge on the right until you reach the next stile. Cross it and walk ahead. Although people seem to continue along the field edge from here, the right of way (shown on the map) bears slightly right across the field to the brow. It then continues in a similar direction to a gate which stands to the right of a brick barn, a feature which is not seen until the brow is reached.*

3. *Go left along the lane. At the crossroads go ahead until you reach the bridge over the Coventry Canal. Go right down to the towpath and walk ahead until you reach Fradley Junction. Cross over the lock by Wharf House to the village and The Swan public house.*

4. *Retrace your steps to the Coventry Canal and walk to Fradley, passing beneath Bridge 90 and Fradley Bridge (91). Soon after look for a little gate on the left by cottages. Go left along the track to a white gate where you bear right to follow a track through to a drive. Pass by the houses up to the main road and school.*

Secluded pool at Chasewater

Chasewater

Outline
Chasewater Visitor Centre − Chasetown − Norton − Chasewater Light Railway − Visitor Centre

Summary
An easy ramble along paths and tracks which have been developed around the waters of Chasewater. This is a classic example of what can be done to change an industrial zone of the past into a leisure facility for the future if everyone takes care of emerging countryside where pits and factories once stood.

Attractions
Chasewater itself is the main attraction and is extremely popular for sailing and water sports during the summer months. There is a large playground near to the Visitor Centre and several open spaces around the water's edge, where the wildfowl can be observed from close quarters. The reservoir was built to serve the extensive local canal system during the late 18th century, but many of the navigations have since gone into disrepair.

The Chasewater Light Railway: This little leisure line, offering return 3 mile steam hauled train trips, was re-opened in 1986 using an old colliery line built by the Marquis of Anglesey to transport coal to the Black Country. The work continues to extend the line towards Chase Terrace, but the current terminus near the lake makes it ideal for a return trip back towards Brownhills for those wishing to finish the walk at a half-way point. Trains run on Sundays and Bank Holidays.

To the south of Chasewater are Brownhills and Clayhanger Commons, which are equally popular for short rambles.

Refreshments
There are refreshments available at Chasewater and at the railway at weekends and on most days during the summer season.

Public Transport
The 156 Birmingham to Cannock and the 345/349 Walsall to Cannock buses offer a good service on Mondays to Saturdays.

Route 5

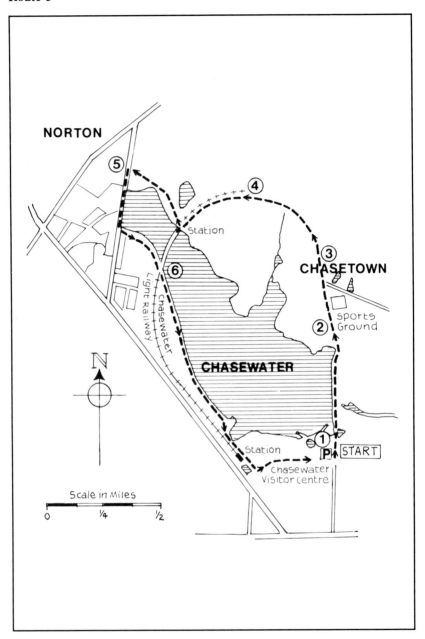

Route 5

Chasewater   4 miles

Start

The Visitor Centre and Picnic Area, Chasewater (OS Landranger Sheets 128 and 139, GR 038071).

Route

1. *Leave the Chasewater car park to turn left along a road. Pass by pools to your right where moorhen and swan are often seen. Cross the bridge over a water channel to rise up to a path which runs along the dam wall.*

2. *This soon drops down to a road again. Go left and cut across rough ground. Head for a corner where the road bends left. However, you bear right to follow a track near to a school ground on your right.*

3. *Pass through a car park and cross a road. Then follow the aggregate track opposite past a club room. The track runs by a grassy enclosure and rises through scrub before dropping to a crossroads of paths.*

4. *Go left here to walk parallel (but at a higher level) to the old railway trackbed, which is being restored by the Chasewater Railway Company. There's a reservoir to your right. The path bears right and on reaching a fork go left to walk through to Norton East Road.*

5. *Go left to walk along the road. Go over a bridge and then turn left to re-enter the parkland. Go right and then follow the path as it cuts left to run alongside the water's edge.*

6. *Cross the railway and walk along an asphalt road. You reach a gate. Go through it and continue ahead on the road to the Chasewater Light Railway station and Colliery Line. Go left at the junction to return alongside a road which leads back to the playground and Visitor Centre.*

Alvecote Priory

Alvecote Pools and railway from the former mine spoil heap

Alvecote Priory and Pools

Outline

Alvecote Priory Picnic Area – Coventry Canal – Amington – Shuttington – Alvecote Priory Picnic Area.

Summary

An easy ramble, straying into Staffordshire, with some road walking, but mainly along a canal towpath and level fieldpaths. The climb to Shuttington village can be avoided by a short cut, saving about $\frac{3}{4}$ mile. From the picnic area, we follow the Coventry Canal west to Amington, before looping round through the fields north of the pools to reach Shuttington by climbing meadows reclaimed from opencast coal mining. The walk returns to the picnic area by road, via the former mining village of Alvecote. A second circular ramble of about one mile can be taken round the neighbouring Warwickshire Wildlife Trust's reserve.

Attractions

The picnic area established by Warwickshire County Council at Alvecote Priory, near the Staffordshire border, is an excellent place for starting a ramble – or for delaying the start of one on a fine summer's day, when sitting or playing on the grass may have a strong appeal.

The small Benedictine priory was established by William Burdet in 1159 as a Cell to Great Malvern Priory, and was dissolved by Henry VIII in 1536. Not much remains, most of the buildings having been pulled down about the year 1700, but there is a good moulded doorway from the late 14th century and a stone dovecote by the canal. The monks kept pigeons there for fresh winter meat, as well as for eggs and fertilizer. Before root crops for animal feeding were developed in the 18th century there were thousands of dovecotes in England.

Across the canal is the Alvecote Pools Nature Reserve, a Site of Special Scientific Interest. Owned by British Coal and leased to Warwickshire Wildlife Trust, it can be visited as an extension to the walk (see Route paragraph 7).

The large pools at Alvecote were formed by mining subsidence during World War II. They are noted for their variety of bird and plant life. One of Britain's first nature trails was set up here in 1963, and there are guided walks during certain summer weekends (tel. 01926 496848).

The Coventry Canal was an early waterway, partly opened in 1769. The section walked had to wait until 1790 for its first traffic, after which it became one of Britain's most profitable canals. Walking its towpath westwards, we pass a marina. Beyond, note the contrast between the wild strip of land between the canal and the railway on one side and the trim golf course across the water. We also pass the buttresses of a former railway bridge that crossed the canal to a mine.

Shuttington village stands high above the Anker valley. Its little old stone

Continued on page 36

Route 6

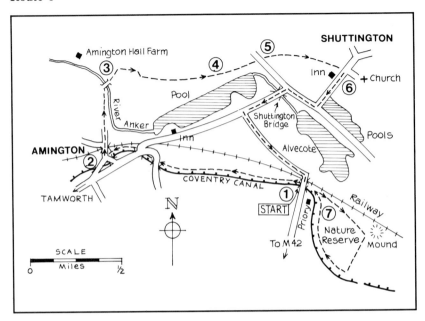

Alvecote Priory and Pools   4 miles or 5 miles

Start

   Alvecote Priory Picnic Area, 3 miles east of Tamworth, where a lane crosses the Coventry Canal and the railway (OS Sheets 139 and 140 GR 250043).

Route

1. *Go out to the road and cross the canal bridge. Descending to the right, turn under the bridge to follow the towpath west for $1\frac{1}{4}$ miles.*

2. *At Bridge No. 65 leave the canal and bear right to a little green, backed by cottages. Go right and follow Moor Lane over a railway bridge. Ignore a left turn and keep ahead along an unmade road ending at a stile. Beyond, veer right towards the River Anker and cross it via the footbridge. Downstream the gabled Amington Hall Farm can be seen.*

3. *Follow the right-hand field-edge to a bend on a concrete drive. Climb a stile and turn right to walk along a green track left of a hedge. Stay on the headland path, which swings right and left to reach a stile/gate and continues beside a wire fence. Away to the right is one of the great pools caused by mining subsidence.*

Route 6 (continued)

4. *Where the fence bears left, keep ahead to a small oak. Passing a pile of rubble on your right (all that remains of Warren Farm), skirt left of woodland and climb a stile. Bear right and walk beside the pool to a lane, where a car-park occupies the site of the former Laundry Cottages. (A short cut can be made here by turning right along the lane and right again on rejoining the longer walk at the next junction.)*

5. *Cross the lane to a gate/stile. Bear sharp right over the field to a gate and climb to a gate on the right. Cross a large field to a stile near the right-hand end of buildings at Shuttington, and step over another stile to gain the road by the Wolferstan Arms. (Opposite, a track leads to the churchyard, with its magnificent view of the Alvecote Pools.)*

6. *Take the roadside footpath downhill past the inn, turn right at the T-junction, and left over Shuttington Bridge. Bear left through Alvecote and go over the railway and canal to return to the picnic site.*

7. *For a second circuit of about a mile, starting from the canal bridge, take the public footpath through the Warwickshire Wildlife Trust's nature reserve. On emerging from the trees, it is worth making a diversion along a left-hand path to climb the spoil heap for its all-round views. To continue, however, turn right here. At a cross-track go right for a few yards, then off left and down to cross a footbridge. Follow the path through trees and, soon climbing to the canal bank, walk it to the right, back to the road bridge.*

Access by bus
Mercian service: Tamworth – Amington – Shuttington.

church contains a Norman doorway brought from Alvecote Priory, and the churchyard provides a magnificent view of the pools. Along the nature reserve circuit notice the stunted oaks and, on the spoil heap, look for black wolf spiders – became an arachnidophile!

Refreshments
The Wolferstan Arms, Shuttington (bar meals). Village stores at Shuttington and Alvecote.

Lord Donegal's Ride and the Ebrook (route 7)

Sutton Park

Outline

Town Gate – Holly Hurst – Jamboree Memorial – Rowton's Hill – Icknield Street – Streetly Gate – Bracebridge Pool – Blackroot Pool – Town Gate.

Summary

A walk through the heathland, woods and wetlands making up the 2,400 acres of one of Britain's largest urban parks, designated as a Site of Special Scientific Interest. The hills are small and gentle, we visit three of the Park's half-dozen large pools, and there are opportunities for refreshments and toilet stops. Though all facilities may not be open in winter, the Park's ease of access to the vast Birmingham and Black Country population makes it especially suitable for walking during the shorter days, and its abundance of holly (but not for picking, please!) adds to the seasonal flavour of a Christmas stroll.

Attractions

Nearly 500 years after Bishop Vesey of Exeter – a local Sutton lad who had made good – persuaded Henry VIII to grant a royal charter to Sutton Coldfield, Sutton Park remains a green oasis within the built-up West Midlands. It is large enough to attract the serious rambler, as well as the stroller content with a circuit of around a mile or so.

The Park was once a royal forest, or hunting ground for the king. In 1126 it came into the ownership of the Earl of Warwick and, being no longer royal, was downgraded from "forest" to "chase". Under Henry VIII's royal charter of 1528, the chase was given to the townspeople of Sutton Coldfield for ever. In the 18th century the Park survived a proposal by Sir Joseph Scott of Great Barr Hall that it should be enclosed and divided up between local landowners, but Victorian conservationists were less successful in 1879 when, amid great controversy, the Midland Railway Company's Birmingham to Walsall line was driven through its north-eastern fringe. Fortunately the scars on the landscape have long since healed and the railway now seems part of the scenery.

In 1957 the World Jubilee Jamboree of the Scout Movement was held in the Park. We pass its commemorative plaque on our walk.

Other features of interest include the Roman road, Icknield Street, which follows the western edge of the Park as part of its journey from Gloucestershire to Yorkshire, and Rowton's Well. We can imagine Roman legionaries camping on nearby Rowton's Hill and using the well, which can be seen within wooden fencing about 300 yards to the south. Between the hill and Icknield Street we follow Lord Donegal's Ride. His lordship lived at Fisherwick Hall, near Lichfield, in the 18th century and used the Ride when hunting in the Park. The Ride passes the Butts, an

Continued on page 40

Route 7

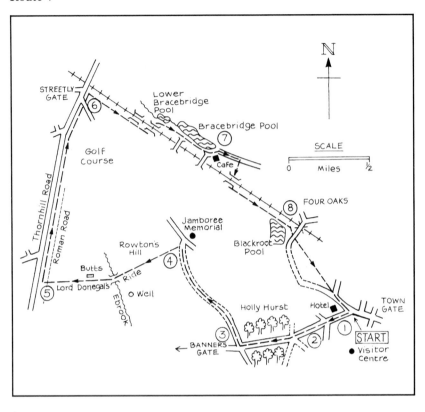

Route 7

Sutton Park
$6\frac{1}{2}$ miles

Start

Town Gate, Tudor Hill, Sutton Coldfield (OS Sheet 139 GR 116964; 6" to 1 mile Map of Sutton Park).

Route

1. Enter Town Gate and, if travelling by car, park within (free). Continue on foot along the road and fork left for 300 yards to a wooden gate barring vehicles. Away to the left is the circular Visitor Centre.

2. Follow the "Pedestrians Banners Gate" pointer ahead and take the surfaced way to the wooded Holly Hurst. At the 5-way junction go straight ahead to climb the broad Wyndley Glade.

3. Emerging from the trees at a cross-roads, turn right along a surfaced way, passing a vehicle barrier and continuing between woods and heathland. Just beyond another vehicle barrier is the Scout Jamboree Memorial.

4. Turn left along a broad, straight track through silver birches to Rowton's Hill, with the distant, pine-capped Barr Beacon visible slightly to the right. Descend the track ahead (Lord Donegal's Ride), cross a bridge over the Ebrook and pass the Butts on your right.

5. About 100 yards before Royal Oak Gate, cross the slightly raised Icknield Street (Roman road). Continue and turn right along the perimeter path, skirting the golf course opened in 1893, to reach Streetly Gate (toilets).

6. Cross the road and bear right beside railway lines. Go left through the second railway arch to Lower Bracebridge Pool. Turn right and take a broad track, with the main Bracebridge Pool glimpsed through trees. Turn left beside the end of the pool to a cafe, refreshment kiosk and toilets, noting the information board along the way.

7. Beyond the cafe follow the road to a parking area. Descend a rough track to your right, pass under a railway arch and turn left to reach Blackroot Pool.

8. Keeping left of the pool, cross a road and veer to the right over high grassland (the site of a Victorian race-course). Descend to Holly Knoll car park and bear left along the road back to Town Gate, passing the entrance to Park House Hotel.

old concrete trench amid pine trees on its north side, used for rifle training by the Army in Victorian times and during World War I. There is a great deal of history to stimulate the mind whilst we walk in the lovely and peaceful acres of Sutton Park.

Refreshments
Park House, near Town Gate; Bobby Brown's Cafe and kiosk, by Bracebridge Pool.

Guidebook
Sutton Park: Its History and Wildlife by Douglas V. Jones. Westwood Press Publications.

Access by train and bus
Trains (Birmingham New Street–Lichfield line) to Sutton Coldfield Station, ¼-mile from Town Gate.
    Buses, WMT services run from the City Centre and many other points to Sutton Coldfield, for Town Gate, and to other gates of the Park.

Kingsbury Church and Manor across Hemlingford Water

40

Kingsbury Water Park

Outline

Visitor Centre – Bodymoor Heath Water – Kingsbury Church – River Tame – Far Leys Car-park – Pools – Birmingham & Fazeley Canal – Broomycroft Car-park – Pools – Woodland Walk – Visitor Centre.

Summary

Level walking on good paths between pools and by the River Tame, and along the Birmingham & Fazeley Canal towpath, but there is a long flight of steps to climb for the optional diversion to Kingsbury Church. Included in the ramble is the Water Park's $1\frac{1}{2}$ mile Winter Walk circuit, which is fully described in a booklet on sale at the shop near the main entrance. The Park's *Find Your Way Around* leaflet, which includes an 8″ to 1 mile map, is useful for this walk.

Bus travellers

Alight in Kingsbury village and join the walk at the church.

Attractions

There are more than 30 lakes and pools in the 600-acre Kingsbury Water Park, which Warwickshire County Council has been developing since 1973 in the Tame valley, between Birmingham and Tamworth. The result of half-a-century of gravel extraction, now landscaped and set among grass and trees, they attract both humans and wildlife.

For a family day out, the Water Park offers miles of waterside and woodland walks, plus games and picnic areas, an adventure playground, boating pools, a visitor centre and cafe (not open in winter), exhibitions and a shop. Make a day of it and combine the short walk described overleaf with enjoyment of the Park's other facilities. The shop sells useful leaflets, including a description of a nature trail opened by TV naturalist Phil Drabble in 1990, and there are guide booklets describing walks for each of the four seasons.

On the walk there is free childrens' fishing and an adventure playground at Far Leys, plus boating on nearby Mitchells Pool. Overlooking the large, irregularly shaped Cliff Pool are wooden hides from which visitors can watch the many birds on the water without disturbing them. The embankment round the pool was constructed to screen the wildfowl from human interference.

The Birmingham & Fazeley Canal was designed by the engineer John Smeaton and completed in 1789. It is a link canal, connecting Birmingham City Centre with the Coventry Canal at Fazeley, near Tamworth, and with the Trent & Mersey at Fradley Junction. Curdworth Bottom Lock, which we pass, is the first of 13, heading south, that raise the level 76 feet in $2\frac{1}{2}$ miles. The lock-keeper's cottage is

Continued on page 44

Route 8

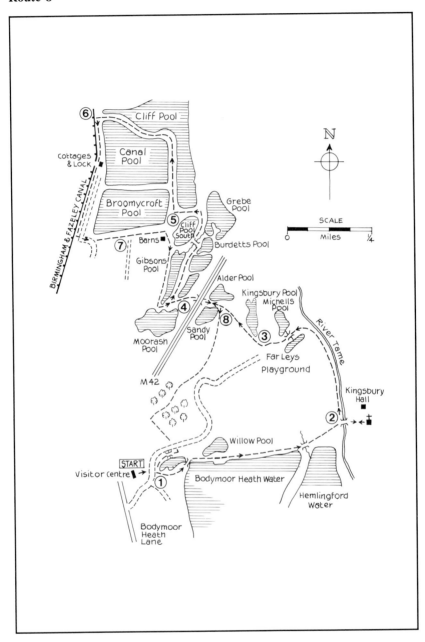

Route 8

Kingsbury Water Park

4 or $1\frac{3}{4}$ miles

Start

Visitor Centre pay car-park, off Bodymoor Heath Lane, between A4091 and A4097 (OS Sheet 139 GR 204959), or free car-park, Pear Tree Avenue, Kingsbury village (GR 218965).

Route

1. *Cross the drive and pick up a gravel path skirting left of Bodymoor Heath Water. Cross a footbridge and follow a causeway to a bridge over the River Tame. Beyond, steps rise to Kingsbury churchyard, and the Elizabethan manor to the north.*

2. *Return and recross the river, bearing right along its bank. Go left between two pools to a railed footbridge and continue across grassland to a track leading to Far Leys car-park and adventure playground.*

3. *Just before the car-park turn right along a broad path. Pass Kingsbury Pool. (* **For a short cut** *reducing the walk to $1\frac{3}{4}$ miles, turn sharp left, following the Woodland Walk – see paragraph 8). Go between Alder and Sandy pools (all names are signposted) to a tunnel under the M42.*

4. *Emerging, keep ahead, then turn right between Burdetts and Gibsons pools. In just under $\frac{1}{4}$ mile cross a railed bridge on the left to Cliff Pool South. Here join the Winter Walk, following it anti-clockwise round the pool to Waymark 4.*

5. *The trail bears right, between the embanked Cliff Pool and Broomycroft Pool, then skirts Canal Pool. Turn left at the end, passing bird-watchers' hides, and follow the shore to the Birmingham & Fazeley Canal.*

6. *Go left along the towpath, past the cottages at Curdworth Bottom Lock, and at Waymark 6 join the access road. Follow it to a right-hand bend, go straight ahead over a stile and continue along a gravel path to Broomy Croft Rare Breeds Farm and Granary Tea Rooms.*

7. *Keep ahead past Waymark 1 to Waymark 2 at Cliff Pool South and bear right, passing 18th century barns. At Waymark 7 turn right, between Gibsons Pool and a meadow, then left to return through the M42 tunnel.*

8. *Beyond Sandy Pool take a path on the right, following the Woodland Walk and emerging from the trees to pass near a bend in a drive. Keep to the path, which meanders through more woodland and meets the drive further south. Cross to a path running parallel to the drive and go over a bridge to the right. The path now curves to the left and leads back to the Visitor Centre.*

43

dated MDCCCXX (1820) in Roman numerals – our modern high-tech age could not have developed if the Arabs hadn't devised our present system of numbers!

The eastern side of the Water Park is bordered by the broad River Tame, which flows north through Tamworth to feed the Trent. Silhouetted on a bank high above it is Kingsbury's great church of Norman origin. Its doorway is of that period, but the tower is 14th century and the belfry was built 200 years later. Beside the churchyard is the long stone wall of the Elizabethan hall, now a farmhouse, where the Saxon kings of Mercia are said to have built a palace.

Refreshments
Café at Visitor Centre in summer; inns (bar meals) at Kingsbury village. Granary Tea Rooms at Broomy Croft.

Access by bus
Mercian service: Birmingham – Kingsbury village – Tamworth.

Kingsbury Manor

44

Hartshill Hayes and the Centenary Way

Outline

Hartshill Hayes Country Park – Ansley Common – Church End – Hoar Park Wood – Birchley Heath – Hartshill Hayes.

Summary

A rather hilly walk, mostly waymarked. It is somewhat longer than other walks, but includes fine elevated stretches and can be greatly shortened, as indicated in the route description. From Hartshill Hayes Country Park, between Nuneaton and Atherstone, a section of the Centenary Way long-distance footpath leads to the former mining village of Ansley Common. We climb fields and join the B4114 to Church End, continuing to Hoar Park Wood, from which we return along the Centenary Way to our starting point.

Attractions

From the county council's Hartshill Hayes Country Park there are immense views north, across the Anker valley, to the rocky tors of Charnwood Forest in Leicestershire. It is said that forty churches can be seen from the hilltop. How many can you count?

The 550ft-high ridge attracted dwellers in the Stone and Bronze ages, when it stood clear and dry above the lowland forests and marshes. There are signs of a hill-fort constructed by the Celts in the centuries before Christ, and in 1125 Hugh de Hardreshull built a castle there.

The 100-mile Centenary Way footpath commemorates the hundredth anniversary of the county council in 1989. Starting from Kingsbury Water Park (see Route 3) the waymarked path winds south to the edge of the Cotswolds at Meon Hill. Guide leaflets to it can be purchased at the Country Park.

Look out for unusual animals at Moorwood Rare Breed Leisure Farm. The ancient church at Church End was once owned by Lady Godiva, and our fieldpath from it leads to Ansley Mill, which occupies a mill site used since the 12th century. Hoar Park Wood is a surviving fragment of the ancient Forest of Arden and a Site of Special Scientific Interest.

Refreshments

Hartshill Hayes Country Park (when ranger present).

Route 9

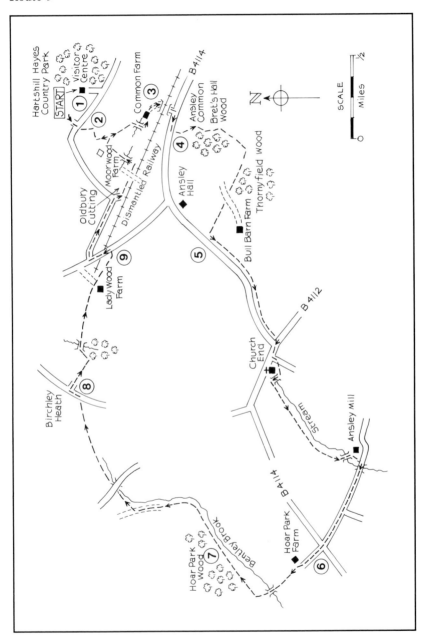

Route 9

Hartshill Hayes and the Centenary Way $3\frac{1}{4}$ miles or 9 miles

Start

Pay car-park at Hartshill Hayes Country Park, $3\frac{1}{2}$ miles north-west of Nuneaton (OS Sheet 140 GR 315946).

Route

1. *From the Visitor Centre follow the St Lawrence Walk's direction post No. 1, at the far side of the car-park. Skirt a covered reservoir on your left and turn left through a gate to a lane.*

2. *From a stile opposite, cross the field diagonally and go over a rise to a stile. Descend an enclosed path towards Moorwood Farm, then turn left along a fenced track, passing a narrow pool. Bearing right to a stile, gate and second stile, cross the end of a field to a stile and short plank footbridge. In the next field go left along the hedge and turn right at the corner to a stile on the left. Cross it and bear right to a stile at Common Farm.*

3. *Follow the farm drive under the railway bridge to Ansley Common, a former mining village on the B4114, and turn right along the roadside footpath for 200 yards. (**For a short cut** reducing the walk to $3\frac{1}{4}$ miles, continue for another $\frac{1}{2}$ mile alongside the B4114 and turn right into a lane. After a further $\frac{1}{2}$ mile rejoin the longer walk just before the turn to Oldbury Cutting Picnic Area – see paragraph 9.)*

4. *For the longer walk, follow the Centenary Way sign left at Limes Coppice to a stile and climb to the left to reach a stile in the projecting upper hedge. Ascend left of a hedge and, where it ends, veer right to a stile in the facing hedge. Skirt Bret's Hall Wood to a gate/stile on the right and descend a field to a stile. Here leave the Centenary Way by climbing the next field to a gate 120 yards from its top-left corner. Turn right along the far side of the hedge to a gate/stile by Thornyfield Wood. Follow the field-edge past the wood and over a stile. Go through the field beyond, aiming for a stile on the B4114, right of woodland.*

5. *Follow the roadside footpath left to Church End. Walk through the churchyard to a stile and cross a railed footbridge. Follow the stream, left, to Ansley Mill, passing woodlands and a pond, and crossing another railed bridge. At the mill cross a plank footbridge and a stile, and bear right to a stile on a lane. Turn right to the B4114.*

6. *Cross the B4114 and descend Hoar Park Farm drive, passing left of the farmhouse to a gate. Turn left down a large field to reach doublegates and a bridge over Bentley Brook, and climb to the corner of Hoar Park Wood, rejoining the Centenary Way and bearing right along it.*

Continued on page 48

7. *Beyond a railed bridge, change sides of the hedge at a stile. Cross more stiles and follow the right-hand edge of a vast field. Go through a gate to join a track for just over 200 yards, take a signed path from a stile on the right and follow a field-edge to a lane. Turn briefly right to a bend and left through a fieldgate. Soon descend steps to an old pack-horse trail leading to another former mining village, Birchley Heath.*

8. *There, turn left along the lane, and take the first road on the right. At the end continue beside a hedge to a wood. Bear left to a stile, and cross a field corner to a plank footbridge and stile. Go down a long field to Lady Wood Farm and over its drive to a stile and signed path, leading to a stile on the left. Cross a field to a stile on a lane, where the shorter walk comes in from the right.*

9. *Turn left, then first right to Oldbury Cutting Picnic Area, where the Centenary Way is signed along a former colliery railway embankment. After climbing the third stile, take a stile on the left with a white waymark, indicating a concessionary path. Descend to cross a plank footbridge and stiles. Climb the field right of Moorwood Farm, where the Centenary Way is arrowed, right, along the top hedge to the short plank footbridge and stile mentioned in paragraph 2. From it retrace your steps to the country park.*

Access by train and bus

Train to Nuneaton or Atherstone. Midland Red from Coventry, Nuneaton or Atherstone to Hartshill village (1 mile from country park), or Ansley Common.

Hartshill Hayes Country Park

Over Whitacre and Furnace End

Outline
Over Whitacre Church − Hoar Hall − Furnace End − Over Whitacre

Summary
An interesting, pretty and varied little walk, part on rolling grassland and part on rough grazing by willowy streams. We have a fine church, a mellow old field barn, a chain of lovely clear ponds, a village mentioned in the Domesday Book and a busy little stream. Near the end you meet a sudden surprise. We will not reveal what it is, only say that, of its type, it is amazingly discreet.

The mention of willowy streams and grazing will tell you that there is a muddy bit with cow plop.

Attractions
Over Whitacre is the name of the hilltop settlement where you start and of the parish, yet it is no more than a handful of houses and St Leonard's Church. Nearby, the village of Furnace End has at least a pub and a phone box, and used to have a Post Office. These two little settlements hide, asleep in gently rolling hills.

St Leonard's is simple and compact in red sandstone with a lofty spire on a lofty hill. Locally it is known as the Squire's Church after the magnate who built it in 1766. The detail around the door, the lunette windows and bell openings are rich and interesting. Originally the church had a domed tower and the spire was added in 1850.

Look out for another building in red sandstone, the field barn with weathered clay tile roof typical of the area. This must have been a true barn, an agricultural factory for winnowing grain, with big opposing doors which could be opened to let the breeze separate the grain from the chaff.

The ponds are surprisingly long and wide, coming from such a tiny stream. Wetlands have grown scarce in our countryside and these that remain are valuable wildlife habitat. You can see swans, coots, moorhens, ducks, bulrushes and cressy weeds in the clear water.

At Furnace End there is a little green on the crossroads where a plaque proudly announces that the village appeared in the Domesday Book of 1086. Passing the Post Box, notice that the monarch is not given a number. You can probably work out who and why.

Look out for the water mill which was once involved in iron smelting by the Jennens family. Charles Jennens collaborated with Handel and wrote the libretto for The Messiah. After leaving the village you walk through a narrow field. There is a stream on the right and the dry bed of a stream on the left, which was once the mill stream.

Near the end of the walk you come through a small plantation. The taller trees are

Continued on page 52

49

Route 10

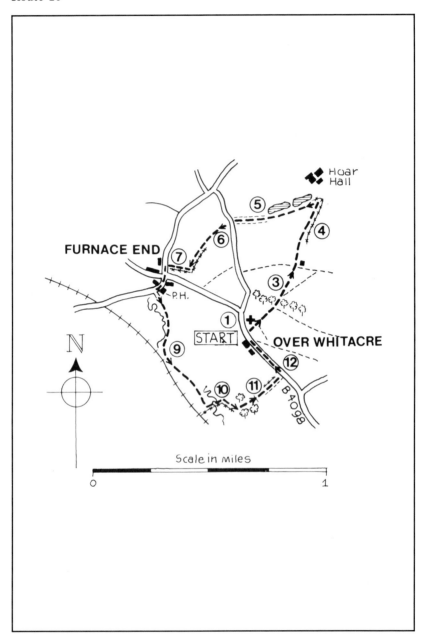

Route 10

Over Whitacre and Furnace End   **3 miles**

Start

Car park of Over Whitacre Parish Hall, by the hilltop church on the B4098 about 1½ miles east of Shustoke. Map reference SP 254910. Landranger Maps: 139 – Birmingham, and 140 – Leicester and Coventry.

Route

1. *From the car park enter the churchyard. Walk down the right side of the church and take the iron kissing gate into a field.*

2. *Turn half left, cross the field and take the stile into a wood. Walk through the wood to a field.*

3. *Go ahead up the field to the left side of the barn. Pass the barn on your right, then head for the bottom right corner of the field and cross a stile.*

4. *Walk with the hedge on your right to the end of the field. (DON'T cross the stile). Go around the field end, and continue with the hedge on your right, via two stiles, to a track.*

5. *Follow the track to a lane. Go left about 350 yards past the first and second gates on your right to cross a stile on the right.*

6. *Follow the left hedge through the fields to the B4114. Go right to the crossroads.*

7. *Turn left and round the right bend to pass the Bull's Head, then just past it take the road left.*

8. *Walk to the end and enter through the wooden garden gate. Go right along the hedge, cross the bridge and take the stile into a narrow field. Walk up the middle to its end, and take the stile by a gate.*

9. *Go ahead between the hedges. As the field widens stay parallel with the railway on your right, to meet a fence and stile. (DON'T cross it). Go down left and cross the footbridge.*

10. *Go right and follow the fence on your right, via a fence gap, and take a stile into the poplar trees. Go left, up the avenue to its top left corner, and cross the stile.*

11. *Walk with the fence on your left to join a track. Continue to its end at the B4098.*

12. *Cross to the footpath and walk left, back to the start.*

St. Leonard's Church, Over Whitacre

Continued from page 49
white poplars, which are native broadleaved trees, but rather common. No lawyer would ever have one in the garden because, without provocation, they shed branches on to neighbours' greenhouses. The trees downhill from the poplars are alders. This waterside tree has short, round female catkins which resemble a tiny fir cone and hang on the tree all winter. The wood was once used to make tool handles and clogs.

Refreshments
The Bull's Head (Free House) in Furnace End offers food.

Public Transport
There is no bus service through Over Whitacre.

Sarehole Mill and the River Cole

Outline

Sarehole Mill – River Cole – Trittiford Mill Park – The Dingles – Sarehole Mill.

Summary

A level walk beside the clear and swift little River Cole and round the lovely Trittiford Mill Pool. It is ideal for families with young children and is possible with pushchairs in dry conditions. The walk can be extended along the river to the south of Scriber's Lane and to the north of Sarehole Mill. The *Birmingham A–Z* will be useful.

Attractions

The ground covered by the walk is a remarkable example of how channels of greenery can survive within industrial cities. At the turn of the century, when J. R. R. Tolkien, author of *The Hobbit* and *The Lord of the Rings*, lived as a child in what is now Wake Green Road, the areas was still rural, and he has described how memories of it influenced him when writing his highly popular books. After the opening of the Birmingham to Stratford railway line in 1907, the city suburbs flowed south to engulf most of the fields and woods. Fortunately some green patches remain to give us an idea of the countryside Tolkien knew. The city council is promoting the Cole Valley as a walkway, both here, in its western section between the Ackers Trust and Yardley Wood, and to the east under Project Kingfisher, between Stechford and Bacon's End.

Sarehole Mill is one of the few places in Hall Green that Tolkien would recognise today. A restored 18th century water-mill, it belongs to the city council and is among the handful of survivors from more than seventy mills once operating in the Birmingham area. As is often the case, a mill existed on the site long before the present buildings were constructed. They date from the 1760s and ended their commercial life in 1919. The 1960s saw them restored as a working mill, and today channels of flowing water and numerous massive, revolving wheels can be seen. The water's source is a large pond behind the mill. Old tools, pictures and displays illustrate the history and techniques of milling.

Children can now be taken to Sarehole Mill without experiencing the fright that young Tolkien had on seeing the father and son who then operated it. He later described them as "characters of wonder and terror to a small child", and remembered how the father had a black beard, though the son – a "white ogre" in his clothes covered with flour dust – was far more frightening. The mill is open from 2 to 5 pm, late March to end of October. Admission free.

The late comedian Tony Hancock was born nearby at 41 Southam Road. Go

Continued on page 56

53

Route 11

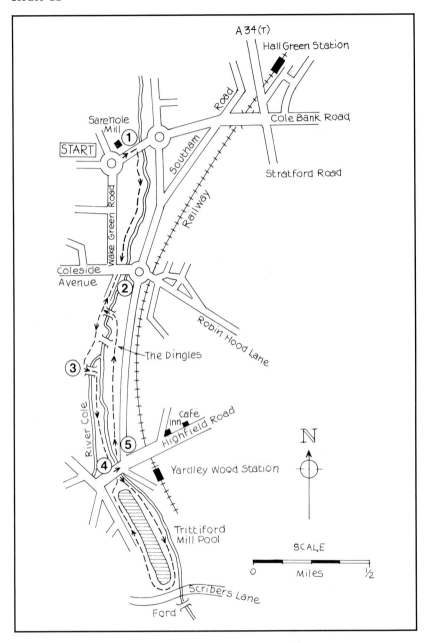

Route 11

Sarehole Mill and the River Cole   3 miles

Start

> *From free car-park, Sarehole Mill Recreation Ground, Cole Bank Road,*
> *Hall Green, Birmingham (OS Sheet 139 GR 099818; Birmingham A–Z).*

Route

1. *Go out to the road and turn right for Sarehole Mill. After visiting the mill, cross the road and take the gravel path opposite the car-park, which meanders through the Cole valley beside the river, to Robin Hood Lane. (A few yards to the right, in Wake Green Road, a row of post-World War II "pre-fabs" can still be seen – a rare survival.)*

2. *Cross Robin Hood Lane to Coleside Avenue, a cul-de-sac, and walk along it. At the end, pass Four Arches Bridge on your left (you will cross it from the other side later), and skirt right of trees. Pass a second bridge, follow the path down an avenue between trees and continue through a broad green area to a railed footbridge on the left.*

3. *Cross the bridge and turn right along a path, with water flowing on each side (a mill-race was constructed in the 18th century to increase the supply to Sarehole Mill), leading to Highfield Road. (Families with pushchairs will find the going easier if they ignore the bridge and continue through the grassy area to the road.)*

4. *Cross the road and the grass beyond it to reach the long, narrow Trittiford Mill Pool. Walk clockwise round the water to Scriber's Lane at the far end, and turn left to visit the ford. Return to the pool and complete the circuit of it through Trittiford Mill Park to Highfield Road.*

5. *Cross to the right of the River Cole and walk beside it through the long green strip known as The Dingles. At the far end, return to Coleside Avenue via Four Arches Bridge (a brick structure resembling an old pack-horse bridge) on your left, and follow the outward route back to Sarehole Mill.*

Access by train and bus

Trains (Birmingham Snow Hill–Stratford line) to Hall Green, $\frac{1}{2}$ mile from Sarehole Mill, or Yardley Wood, 300 yards from River Cole in Highfield Road.

Buses WMT services from the city centre and along the Outer Circle to Cole Bank Road.

left from Sarehole Mill along Cole Bank Road, cross Sarehole Road to Southam Road and turn left to No. 41 on the far side (plaque on wall).

Trees and shrubs line the river between Sarehole Mill and Trittiford Mill Pool, and in the long green meadows there is evidence of an old ridge and furrow system.

Though it long ago lost its mill, Trittiford Mill Pool has a lovely, wooded setting and is noted for its bird life. The ford in Scriber's Lane, at its southern end, is an unusual feature for a modern city suburb.

Refreshments
Pub and cafe in Highfield Road, east of River Cole.

The ford, Scriber's Lane

56

Route 12 $5\frac{1}{2}$ **miles**

Knowle and Temple Balsall

Outline
Knowle – Barston – Temple Balsall – Knowle.

Summary
A walk on fieldpaths, a canal towpath and quiet lanes through gently undulating countryside to the east of Knowle. We climb to the churchyard at Barston for its wide-ranging views (there is a useful seat for a coffee or lunch break, and a nearby inn), and visit impressive old almshouses and the church of the Knights Templar at Temple Balsall. Wellies are recommended after prolonged wet weather, because fields near the River Blythe can flood, as can part of the green lane from Piercil End.

Attractions
Gypsies, navvies and medieval knights are our companions on this ramble. We meet the first at Knowle, where the magnificent church, dating from 1402, has the tomb of a gypsy king, Lawrence Boswell, and his son of the same name, outside its south wall. Only rarely can an ancient church be so precisely dated, but we know that it was built by locally-born Walter Cook, who had risen to be a Canon of the Church and a wealthy man. He also paid for the fine Guild House next door.

The navvies (short for navigators) built Britain's network of canals in the late 18th and early 19th centuries. We see some of their work when walking the towpath of the Grand Union Canal. The Grand Union Canal Company was formed in 1929 by combining several canals. The section we follow was originally part of the Warwick & Birmingham Canal, opened in 1800.

Temple Balsall is an exciting place for anybody with a historical imagination, and a lovely one even to those who lack it. For between the quadrangle of almshouses for poor women – the Lady Katherine Leveson Hospital of 1678 – and the Old Hall stands the great church of the Knights Templar (or, perhaps, of their successors the Hospitallers). Also known as the Knights of St John, the Hospitallers were the forerunners of today's St John's Ambulance Brigade. The Templars were a band of soldier priests formed in 1118 to protect pilgrims to the Holy Land, and as such fought in the Crusades. They acquired land at Balsall in 1146 and it became one of their major bases until the order was disbanded in 1308. Their possessions were transferred by order of the Pope to the Hospitallers, who remained at Temple Balsall until about 1470. The church was restored in the late 1840s. Its varying floor levels are unusual, as is the lack of aisles and transepts in so large a building.

The Old Hall is a survival of the Hospitallers' days. Lady Katherine Leveson, who endowed the hospital, was a grand-daughter of Queen Elizabeth's Robert Dudley, Earl of Leicester, who lived at Kenilworth Castle. The path we follow from the almshouses to the Old Hall is known as The Breadwalk, because the women used it when collecting their bread allowance from the bailiff.

57

Route 12

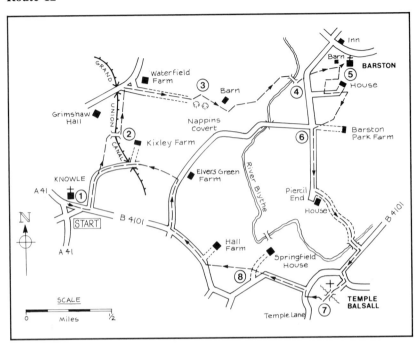

The Breadwalk, with Almshouse entrance on the right

Route 12

Knowle and Temple Balsall   5½ miles

Start

From the parish church at Knowle (OS Sheet 139 GR 182767), or from Kixley Lane (see Route paragraph 1) – roadside parking and small lay-by.

Route

1. *With your back to the church, turn left to follow the minor road away from the village and go left into Kixley Lane. After about ⅓ mile climb a stile on the left, and bear right to a stile in the hedge, then left along a curving field-edge to the Grand Union Canal.*

2. *Cross the high footbridge and follow the towpath left to a roadbridge. Turn right along the road and branch right into Waterfield Farm. Keeping ahead, pass through two sets of double-gates and follow a track between buildings. Becoming a hedged way, it runs along a broad ridge with good views on each side.*

3. *Turn through a gate to go left of Nappins Covert, continue right of a ruined brick barn to a gate, and bear left to a corner stile. Go over the next field diagonally to a gate/stile at the far corner and veer right to cross the River Blythe by a footbridge.*

4. *Turn left, cross a lane via stiles, and climb to a stile between trees. Go up past a barn to a stile on the left, from which a path leads into Barston churchyard. If making for the Bull's Head, take the road to the left for 100 yards.*

5. *Return to the barn and descend to a stile at the bottom right-hand corner of the field. Two more stiles lead to a house drive – there turn left. At a bend continue through a fieldgate and climb a stile on the right by a pool. Veering right to a stile in the facing hedge, turn sharp right to the far field corner, step through a wooden fence and go out to the junction of Hob Lane and Elvers Green Lane.*

6. *Turn left up Hob Lane to Piercil End, and fork left along a green lane to reach the B4101. (If conditions are too wet, return along Hob Lane and go left into Elvers Green Lane to reach the stile indicated in paragraph 8.) Turn right along the B4101 and first left to Temple Balsall. Here, take the path on the right (The Breadwalk) past the almshouses, church and Old Hall.*

7. *Cross a bridge and bear right through a kissing gate to a woodland path. Fork left to reach Temple Lane and turn right for a few yards to the B4101. Go left along it, passing a Warwickshire Wildlife Trust nature reserve and Springfield House (now a school). Leave the road at a left-hand bend, taking a path between holly bushes on the right.*

Continued on page 60

8. *Cross a drive to a stile and follow a right-hand hedge back to the B4101. Bear right along the road, and turn right into Elvers Green Lane. Go along the lane to a signposted gate on the left, just before Elvers Green Farm. Follow the left-hand field-edge to a stile and cross a little footbridge to the next stile. Ahead is a bridge over the Grand Union Canal, with Kixley Lane beyond.*

Access by bus
WMT local services from Solihull to Knowle.

Refreshments
The Bull's Head at Barston (food); teas at Almshouses, Temple Balsall, on summer Saturdays, Sundays and Bank Holidays.

The Almshouses, Temple Balsall

Berkswell and its Windmill

Outline

Berkswell – Baulk Lane – Carol Green – Catchems Corner – Berkswell Windmill – Berkswell Station – Ram Hall – Berkswell.

Summary

An easy circuit, mainly on waymarked fieldpaths, linking the attractive and interesting Berkswell village with Berkswell Windmill. If Berkswell Museum or the windmill are to be visited, the walk must be taken on a summer Sunday afternoon or a Bank Holiday. Allow about 20 minutes for the windmill, but much more for the church and museum.

Attractions

Berkswell village green is bordered on one side by cottages and a shop with Georgian bow windows, and by 19th century almshouses on the other. The old stocks always provoke comment. Why are there five leg holes, rather than six? No one knows, but it has been suggested that they were made for a one-legged lawbreaker and his two companions.

Facing the green are the gates of The Well House, a 17th century former rectory. It was the childhood home of Maud Watson, first winner of the Wimbledon Ladies' Tennis Championship in 1884, who is buried in the churchyard, near the porch. Left of the gates is the large well from which the village took its name. The monks who brought Christianity to the area used it to baptise converts. Beyond the well lie the almshouses' gardens, with access to Berkswell Village Museum. Run by volunteers, it has much interesting local information.

The parish church dates from the 12th century. Unusual features are a double crypt, possibly of Saxon origin, and a 16th century timber-framed priest's room over the porch. But how many mice can you count? There are eleven, the trade marks of woodcarver Robert Thompson.

In the churchyard look out for the broken pillar above the grave of James Owen, which symbolises the cutting off of his head in a gruesome sawmill accident in 1898, and that of James Weetman, who died in 1840 "of a broken heart". It was deliberately placed beside the path, so that the young lady who had trifled with his affections couldn't miss it. On another gravestone are carved 2 loaves, 21 eggs and 18 rashers of bacon – the deceased is said to have expired from overeating.

The Bear Inn has stood at the cross-roads for 400 years. Outside is a Russian cannon captured in 1855 by Captain Arthur Wilmot of Berkswell Hall.

Berkswell Windmill, built in 1826, is a typical Warwickshire tower mill on the site of a much earlier post mill. Its machinery and fittings are complete, though not in working order, but there are plenty of miller's tools to be seen and the sails are in place. The mill ground its last corn in 1948. It was restored in 1973.

Route 13

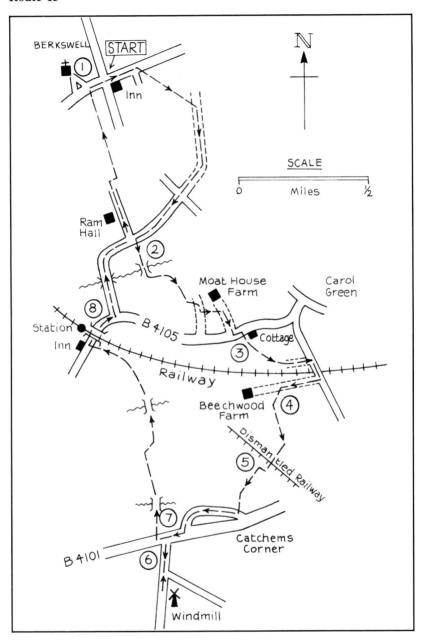

BERKSWELL
START
① + ■ ▷
Inn ■
N
SCALE
0   Miles   ½
Ram ■ Hall
②
Moat House Farm ■
Carol Green
⑧
Station
Inn ■
B 4105
③ ■ Cottage
Railway
④
Beechwood Farm ■
Dismantled Railway
⑤
⑦
B 4101
⑥
Catchems Corner
Windmill

Route 13

Berkswell and its Windmill $5\frac{1}{2}$ miles

Start

Roadside parking space in Meriden Road, Berkswell, or free public car-park near village green (OS Sheets 139 and 140 GR 246791).

Route

1. *From the Bear Inn follow Coventry Road past Pound Close to a stile set back on the right. Go over a rise and between clumps of trees to a stile on a metalled drive. Turn right to Spencers Lane and cross to Baulk Lane.*

2. *Opposite the drive of Ram Hall turn left through a fieldgate and descend to a railed footbridge. Go left to the field-corner and swing right along the hedge to join a track leading to Moat House Farm. At a large oak, about 100 yards before the farm, cross diagonally right to a drive. Turn right for 50 yards to a stile on the left. Follow the ancient moat to a stile/gate, continue to a stile and turn right along a drive to the B4105.*

3. *Go left to Jasmine Cottage, and turn right along a path beside it. Continue over a stile and follow the left-hand field-edges past two more stiles to a railway cutting. From a stile/gate turn left along a track to a road, bear right over the railway and right again into the drive of Beechwood Farm.*

4. *Climb a stile on the left at the end of a hedge and cross to another at the far field corner. Bear left along a track to a stile/gate and follow the right-hand hedge through fields to a dismantled railway.*

5. *Turn right along the top of the embankment for a few steps and descend the far side. Follow the right-hand hedge to join a fenced path leading to Waste Lane at Catchems Corner, and turn right to the B4101. Go right and first left to visit Berkswell Windmill.*

6. *Return to the B4101 and bear left. Immediately beyond a bus shelter on the right, take a path beside the wall of a house to join a gravel drive. Keep ahead along a green track, climb a stile on the left, and turn right along a hedge to a stile.*

7. *Cross the stile and follow the waymarked path over a footbridge, then left of a hedge to a stile/gate. Bear right across a field to a stile in the opposite hedge and follow right-hand field-edges, via a footbridge, to a stile/gate on your right. In the next field turn left and keep on the same line as before, through two gateways, to the B4105, by Berkswell Station. To the left is the Railway Inn.*

Continued on page 64

8. *Go under the railway, re-enter Baulk Lane on your left, and turn left along the drive to the Elizabethan Ram Hall. On the right, opposite the house, is a stile. Cross it, turn left to a gate and descend to a stile/gate. Skirt anti-clockwise, climb a stile at the top right field corner and turn left to follow the far side of the hedge back to Berkswell.*

Access by train and bus

Trains to Berkswell Station (Birmingham New Street–Coventry line). Buses to Berkswell village (WMT Solihull–Coventry services).

Refreshments

The Bear Inn, Berkswell, and the Railway Inn by the station provide bar meals. Stores on B4101, near Berkswell Windmill. Teas on summer Sundays and Bank Holidays at the Reading Room, Meriden Road, Berkswell.

Kenilworth Castle

Route 14

4 miles or 6½ miles

Clowes Wood and Earlswood Lakes

Outline
Clowes Wood – Earlswood Lakes – Salter Street – Lady Lane –
Earlswood Lakes – Clowes Wood.

Summary
The 4 mile walk is on footpaths through Clowes Wood and beside the lovely
Earlswood Lakes. The 2½ mile extension, which mainly follows quiet lanes, passes
near three inns and a village store. Much of the Stratford upon Avon Canal towpath
north of Lapworth has been virtually unwalkable for years, but British Waterways
is in process of opening it up as a walkway from Birmingham to Stratford.
Therefore, walkers using this route may one day find the towpath worth
investigating as an agreeable short cut between Salter Street (B4102) and Lady
Lane. The lakeside paths are also eroded and often muddy – boots or wellies
recommended.

Attractions
The 73 acres of Clowes Wood, together with the adjoining New Fallings Coppice
and Earlswood Lakes, form a Site of Special Scientific Interest. Since 1974 the wood
has been owned and managed as a nature reserve by Warwickshire Wildlife Trust.
Oak, birch, beech, alder and rowan are the main trees found there. Since the ground
is acidic and very wet underfoot in places, it is advisable to keep to the route
described. The nature reserve includes heathland and a 200 years-old hay meadow.

Nearly two centuries after they were constructed, Earlswood Lakes have
become almost natural features of the landscape. Bordered by trees and footpaths
and divided by causeways, the three reservoirs were built in 1810 to supply water to
the Stratford upon Avon Canal. The cost to the canal company of the 51 acres of
Earlswood Common, out of which the great pools were cut, was a mere £969 8s 9d.
Though the Act of Parliament authorising the local canal was passed in 1793, the
company met problems in raising the money for its construction, and the waterway
was not fully opened until 1816. Within twenty years it was feeling the pinch from
the new-fangled railways, and was sold to the Great Western Railway in 1856. Like
most canals, the Stratford upon Avon suffered a long decline until the second half of
the 20th century, when tourist traffic brought a revival.

The original Salter Street Chapel was built in 1840, largely from the money paid
thirty years earlier for the land occupied by the lakes. Its tower was added in 1861
and the rest of the building reconstructed in 1899.

Bedsworth Farm, north of the chapel, was formerly a manor house and is
known to have had its own chapel in 1729.

65

Route 14

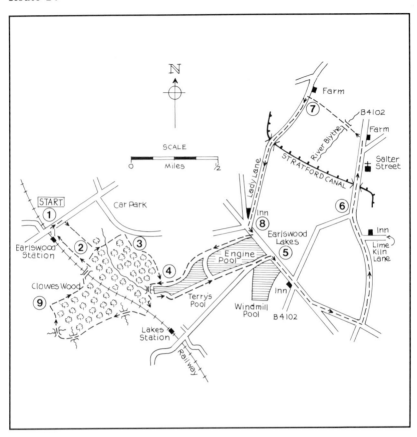

Earlswood Lakes

Route 14

Clowes Wood and Earlswood Lakes

4 miles or $6\frac{1}{2}$ miles

Start

From Earlswood Station (OS Sheet 139 GR 095743), or from Clowes Wood car-park (free) in Wood Lane (GR 102743 – see paragraph 2).

Route

1. *Leaving the station, turn right along the road and take an enclosed path on the right, signed "Clowes Wood". Pass an old moat on your left, enter the wood at a stile, and keep ahead along a path.*

2. *Fork right, go through a clearing and cross a little brook. Follow the main path, keeping near the left-hand edge of the wood and swinging right to the Wood Lane entrance (the motorists' starting point for the walk).*

3. *Step over a wooden fence ahead, and descend to the right alongside the wood (here known as New Fallings Coppice), re-entering it right of a timber building. The path continues through to Terry's Pool, one of the three Earlswood Lakes.*

4. *Walk anti-clockwise round the pool. Pass the causeway, and continue beside Engine Pool. On reaching the road dividing Engine Pool from Windmill Pool, bear left to the dam. Choose now between turning right for the longer walk or left for the shorter one (see paragraph 8 where the routes rejoin).*

5. *The longer walk follows the narrow road to the right along the dam and crosses the B4102 by the Reservoir Inn and the village stores. Fork left at the next junction, and turn left at a cross-roads. After $\frac{1}{2}$ mile pass the end of Lime Kiln Lane (just along which is the Bull's Head) and join the B4102.*

6. *Turn right and follow it over the Stratford upon Avon Canal and past Salter Street Chapel. Beyond a road junction is a signed path from a stile on the left, opposite Bedsworth Farm. Climb the stile and go down a field to a stile/gate, cross the young River Blythe via a concrete culvert and continue to another stile. Beyond it, follow the hedge on your right, via a stile/gate, to a gate on Lady Lane.*

7. *Turn left, recrossing the canal and passing the Red Lion. Bear left at a cross-roads to return to Engine Pool, noting a feeder canal.*

8. *Rejoining the shorter route, bear right of Engine Pool to return to Terry's Pool. After passing the point where you emerged earlier from the woods, turn right over a footbridge and stiles. Cross the railway embankment and follow the waymarked*

Continued on page 68

*path skirting Clowes Wood. Beyond the third footbridge, at a corner of the wood,
the path is arrowed to a stile, then across a field to the next stile. After crossing this,
turn right to a stile/gate leading into the wood.*

9. *Though the right-of-way runs outside the wood, there is a concessionary path
   through – both lead to a footbridge over the railway. Having crossed, to return to
   the station go sharp left along a path running parallel to the line. Otherwise, keep
   ahead along a field-edge to reach the stile into the wood and continue to the Wood
   Lane car-park, as described in paragraph 2.*

Access by train
Earlswood Station (Birmingham Snow Hill to Stratford upon Avon line).

Refreshments
The Reservoir Inn and the nearby village stores, the Bull's Head (children's
playground) and the Red Lion are all on or near the longer route.

Earlswood Lakes

Kenilworth Castle

Kenilworth Castle

Kenilworth Castle and The Pleasance

Outline
Kenilworth Castle – Chase Wood – The Boot Inn – Honiley Church – The Pleasance – Kenilworth Castle.

Summary
The walk mainly follows fieldpaths waymarked by Kenilworth Footpath Preservation Group, which also installed the railed footbridge crossed twice on the 6 mile route. Walkers who prefer to visit Kenilworth Castle in the middle of their ramble, rather than at the beginning or the end, can start from the lane between the Boot Inn and Honiley Church (roadside parking, OS Sheet 139 GR 243722). Since the Castle ruins are substantial, about two hours should be allowed for exploring them.

Attractions
Kenilworth Casle (maintained by English Heritage) was one of England's most impressive buildings during the Middle Ages, and is an exciting place to visit today. Enough of its red sandstone walls remain for us to imagine what it was like at its peak in Queen Elizabeth I's time, when held by her favourite, Robert Dudley, Earl of Leicester. The last of the Queen's three visits there, in 1575, forms the basis of Sir Walter Scott's novel *Kenilworth*.

Visitors enter the site along a causeway from the south car-park. Known as the Tiltyard, it was used for jousting in the late Middle Ages. Imagine how pairs of knights, with lances dressed (*i.e.* at the ready), would have galloped along it, one on either side of a barrier, each determined to unseat the other.

The main buildings within the Castle walls are the massive Keep, begun in the 12th century, and John of Gaunt's Great Hall, built two hundred years later. There are also many lesser ones, including Leicester's Gatehouse and Stables, which house an information display and the English Heritage shop.

In 1265 the Battle of Kenilworth took place, when Edward, son of Henry III, defeated Simon de Montfort the Younger, before going on to beat Simon the Elder at Evesham. In the following year many surviving de Montfort supporters endured a six months' siege at the Castle, before surrendering to the King. In those days, before gunpowder was introduced to Europe, such a mighty fortress was impregnable and its defenders could only be starved out.

After being occupied by Parliamentarian troops during the Civil War, Kenilworth Castle was partly demolished in the 1650s.

To the west of the Castle lay a great Mere. It was expanded during the reign of King John and its northern arm filled the dip in Purlieu Lane (the name of which suggests that it marked an ancient boundary). The Mere was drained in 1650.

Further along our walk, Chase Lane and Chase Wood were named from a 19th century steeplechase.

Continued on page 74

71

Route 15

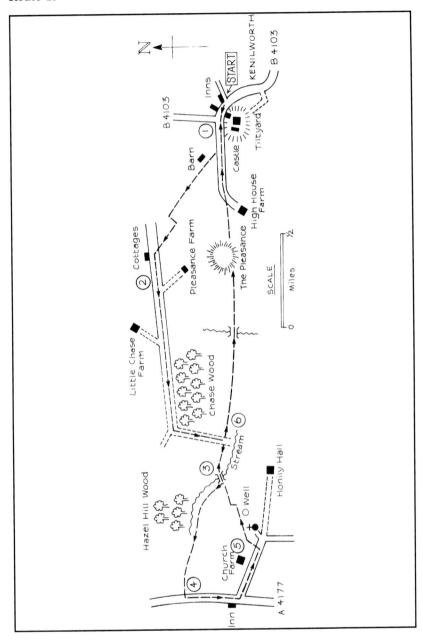

72

Route 15

Kenilworth Castle and The Pleasance

4 miles or 6 miles

Start

Free car-park opposite Castle Green on the B4103 (OS Sheet 140 GR 279724; for the 6 mile route OS Sheet 139 is also required).

Route

1. *From the car-park follow the embankment between the road and the dry moat, and descend to the unsurfaced Purlieu Lane. After about 200 yards climb a stile on the right and ascend to a gate at the far field corner, beyond a brick barn. Go half-left across the next field to a stile, from which the path runs to the far corner of a third field. From an exit stile, follow the right-hand hedge to a stile, and cross to a stile on Chase Lane, opposite cottages.*

2. *Bear left along the lane and continue beside Chase Wood. At the end of the wood turn left, down a broad track at the edge of a long field. (On reaching a path junction at the bottom of the field, choose between a 4 mile and a 6 mile ramble. For the shorter walk, go left, as described in 6 below. For the longer route, which returns to this point, turn right along a field-margin.)*

3. *At the end of the field cross a railed footbridge and bear right, beside Hazel Hill Wood. At the corner take the hedge-gap ahead and follow the right-hand field-edge past a grove of trees. Cross to a marker post where the hedge on the right ends, and go over the next field to a gap beside a tree bearing a direction arrow.*

4. *Turn left along the grassy margin of the A4177 to the Honiley Boot Inn, and take the lane opposite. After about ⅓-mile cross a stile on the left (but first, you may like to continue for 200 yards to see the charming little 18th century Honiley Church).*

5. *From the stile cross to a gap beside a tree stump, and follow a hedge to a waymarked gap on the right. Continue beside another hedge, beyond which is the ancient St John's Well. Descend to a marker post, bear right along a field-edge to the footbridge used earlier, and retrace your steps to the track from Chase Wood, which you previously descended.*

6. *Cross the track and continue down two long field-edges to a railed footbridge. Follow the hedge on the left to a stile, then a hedge on the right to the next stile, and cross the right-hand edge of The Pleasance to a stile. Finally, an enclosed path leads past High House Farm to Purlieu Lane, with its impressive view of the Castle.*

Towards the end of the ramble we pass the site of The Pleasance. It dates from 1414, when Henry V cleared and drained part of the Mere in order to lay out a timber-framed summer house and garden. Two diamond-shaped moats, one within the other, can be seen in the field. Originally they were linked to the Mere by a wide channel, along which boats could approach from the Castle.

Refreshments
Inns at Castle Green, Kenilworth, and at Honiley; shop (pop, ice-cream) at Castle Green; ice-cream at Kenilworth Castle.

Access by bus
Midland Red South services, connecting Coventry, Kenilworth, Leamington Spa, Warwick and Stratford upon Avon, pass Kenilworth Castle.

Stoneleigh Church

74

Stoneleigh and Baginton

Outline

Stoneleigh – River Sowe – Baginton Church – Lunt Roman Fort – Baginton village – Stoneleigh.

Summary

Fieldpath walking beside the little River Sowe, from Stoneleigh to Baginton, returning by quiet lanes. Stoneleigh is a lovely old village, and at Baginton there is a rather quaint church and a reconstructed Roman fort. Aerial activity from Coventry Airport will be of interest , and there may be time to include a visit to the Midland Air Museum at Baginton.

Attractions

At Stoneleigh (originally Stanlei) we pass through riverside meadows and between old houses, including The Cruck Cottage of ancient timber construction, to reach the 700 years-old church. Note the filled-in Norman arch outside the north wall. In the church, which has one of England's finest Norman chancel arches, you can buy an informative guide to the village. The meadows around the church are preserved by a charitable trust. Passing the magnificent gabled Manor Farmhouse in Vicarage Road, we reach The Green, where stand mellow stone almshouses of 1594 and a still-active smithy dated 1851.

Stoneleigh is on the 100-mile Centenary Way walking route, established by the county council to commemorate its hundredth anniversary in 1989. Nearby stands the great Stoneleigh Abbey, its architecture ranging back from the 18th century to early monastic buildings 500 years older. The grounds now house the National Agricultural Centre, where the Royal Agricultural Show is held annually in July.

A pleasant walk through the Sowe valley leads to another old village, Baginton. It entered history briefly one morning in September 1398, when Henry Bolingbroke, Duke of Hereford, rode out from its castle to Gosford Green, now part of Coventry. There, as powerfully portrayed in Shakespeare's *Richard II*, he had a dramatic confrontation with Thomas Mowbray, Duke of Norfolk, when each accused the other of treason. Both were banished by the king, but Bolingbroke returned the following year, forced Richard to surrender and began his reign as Henry IV.

Baginton Castle was then the home of Sir William Bagot, one of the "creatures" (Shakespeare's word) of King Richard. Now a scanty ruin, it lies amid undergrowth next to the rather curious church, which contains fine brasses of Sir William and his lady. In the churchyard are the graves of seven young wartime Polish airmen, who crashed nearby in 1940.

But Baginton has older memories. Lunt Roman Fort dates from about AD60, when Queen Boudica was fighting the new Roman rulers. Its ground-plan can be

Continued on page 78

75

Route 16

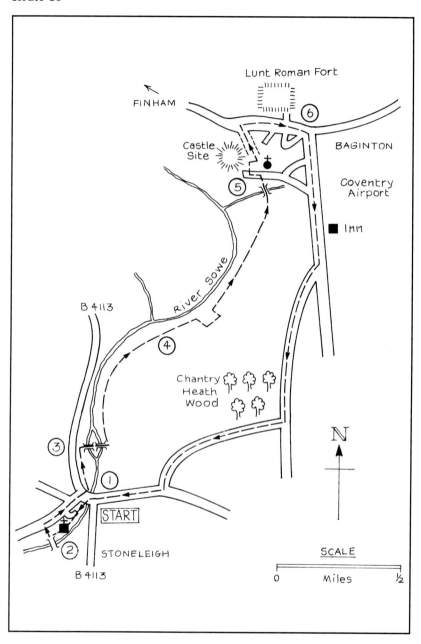

Lunt Roman Fort

FINHAM

Castle Site

BAGINTON

Coventry Airport

■ Inn

River Sowe

B 4113

④

⑤

⑥

Chantry Heath Wood

N

③

①

START

②

STONELEIGH

B 4113

SCALE

0   Miles   ½

76

Route 16

Stoneleigh and Baginton   5 miles

Start

Off-road parking at Stoneleigh (or Rennie) Bridge on B4113 (formerly A444) (OS Sheet 140 GR 333727).

Route

1. *Cross the River Sowe by the bridge and turn left through a gate to a riverside meadow. Follow the right-hand hedge to a gate and take the road ahead, between cottages, to Stoneleigh churchyard.*

2. *Pass through to the far gate, from which a path descends a meadow to a footbridge over the river. Do not cross, but turn right up a drive and right again along Vicarage Road into the village. Continue past The Green to Coventry Road (B4113) and bear left along the footpath beside it.*

3. *After 300 yards, turn right down a signed path from a gate, passing a small brick building. Cross the divided River Sowe by two bridges to reach a meadow, and turn left to a stile/gate. Follow the hedge on your right and, towards the far end of the field, change sides of it at a stile.*

4. *Continue to a corner stile and along a narrow field, then skirt a sewage farm fence to a stile by a large, sawn-off tree-trunk. Descend to the left and go right along the bottom of the field. After four more stiles, the path climbs gently to a stile near a gate. Beyond, cross a footbridge and kissing gate near Pool Cottage, and climb to emerge on a lane, opposite Baginton Church.*

5. *Turn left, and take an arrowed path on the right through the churchyard. A gate leads out to the overgrown site of Baginton Castle. There, turn right along a path to another churchyard gate and bear left, following a path through the overgrown area to a gateway in a tall wooden fence. Keep ahead along a track past a house to a road, Mill Hill, and turn right to Lunt Roman Fort.*

6. *Leaving the fort, continue along the main road (here called Coventry Road). Follow it through a junction, where it swings right to pass the Oak Inn and Coventry Airport. Fork right, and at the next junction, by Chantry Heath Wood, bear right again down a pleasant by-way ending at a T-junction. Stoneleigh Bridge lies downhill, to the right.*

clearly seen, some of the timber buildings were reconstructed by the Royal Engineers in 1971 and there is an interesting museum. The fort is unique in having a *gyrus*, or cavalry training ring. It is believed to have been the main centre for breaking and training horses seized from the Iceni tribe after Boudica's defeat.

Refreshments

The Oak Inn (bar meals), or Coventry Airport Cafe, both at Baginton. None at Stoneleigh.

Access by bus

WMT service: Coventry–Finham ($\frac{1}{2}$ mile from Baginton). Heyfordian Coaches, Banbury: Kenilworth–Stoneleigh service.

The Green, Stoneleigh

Henley's Castle Mount

Outline
Henley in Arden – The Mount – Preston Field Lane – Preston Bagot – Stratford upon Avon Canal – Pettiford Lane – River Alne – Blackford Mill – Henley in Arden.

Summary
Fieldpaths, an old unsurfaced lane, a canal towpath and a riverside path, plus a few short connecting stretches of road make up this varied ramble. The terrain is equally divided between the hilly landscape (by Warwickshire standards) north-east of Henley in Arden and the level walking beside the Stratford upon Avon Canal and the River Alne. Part of the ramble follows the waymarked Heart of England Way, a 100-mile walking route from Cannock Chase to the Cotswolds.

Attractions
This is real "king of the castle" country, for just outside Henley in Arden rises The Mount, on which stood the castle of the powerful de Montfort family. Not a stone remains, but it is easy to imagine how Thurstan de Montfort, at the end of the 11th century, saw its military possibilities. In the castle's first years there was no town below – just the huddled village of Beaudesert ("beautiful wilderness" in the Norman French spoken by those early nobles). But after the granting of a charter in 1140 for a weekly fair and market, Henley began to grow. Its prosperity came to an end in 1265, when the Lord of the Manor, Peter de Montfort, sided with his cousin Simon against Henry III's troops at the Battle of Evesham. The battle was lost and both were killed. The reprisals included partial destruction of the castle.

Henley's other attractions include two old churches standing only 200 yards apart at each end of Beaudesert Lane, the nearby Guild Hall and a 500 years-old broken market cross on High Street, plus many picturesque buildings and the town's most famous product – ice-cream. Though St John's Church at Henley dates – like the Guild Hall – from the mid-15th century, St Nicholas's at Beaudesert is 300 years older.

Along the Stratford upon Avon Canal towpath note the split bridges, built in two halves with a one inch gap between, so that the towropes could pass through without the horses being unhitched.

Buildings of interest include the little Norman hilltop church and the Manor House at Preston Bagot, and Blackford Mill on the River Alne. It is worth stepping into the churchyard for its extensive views. The lovely gabled and half-timbered Manor House, by the B4095, has been converted to apartments. Blackford Mill stands on an ancient mill site. There is a possible reference to it as early as 1296 and the building continued in use as a mill until 1957. It is now a private house, its 15ft waterwheel hidden within brick casing.

Route 17

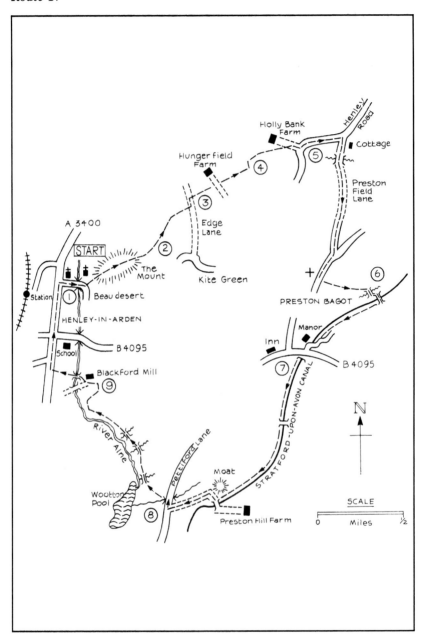

Route 17

Henley's Castle Mount   **7 miles**

Start

Beaudesert Lane, Henley in Arden (OS Sheet 151 GR 151660). Roadside parking in High Street and Beaudesert Lane.

Route

1. *From St John's Church in High Street turn along Beaudesert Lane, passing St Nicholas's Church. Go through a kissing gate, climb the steep path over The Mount and bear left up to three stiles at a field corner.*

2. *Take the left-hand stile (marked "Heart of England Way", which you follow to Henley Road – paragraph 4) along a green track for 400 yards to a stile on the right. Cross a field to a stile, and turn left along Edge Lane, now just a narrow hedged path.*

3. *Turn off right at a stile and, aiming between tall trees, cross a field and the drive of Hungerfield Farm. Descend right of a hedge and, when it bears away, keep ahead to a stile leading into a copse.*

4. *Pass through the copse, climb to a stile in the upper hedge and continue over a rise to a stile right of a line of tall cypresses at Holly Bank Farm. Climb a second stile and go down the field to join the farm drive at a gate, following it out to Henley Road.*

5. *Go left for nearly $\frac{1}{3}$ mile, and turn right into the unsurfaced Preston Field Lane, which, from a bend, angles back past a cottage. Continue to a road junction and bear right to a stile opposite Preston Bagot church. Descend the field to a gate and go down a long, sloping field to a stile/gate at the bottom.*

6. *Cross a stream by a railed footbridge, and follow a fenced path to a split-bridge on the Stratford upon Avon Canal. Go over it and take the towpath to the right. Where it ends, beyond the Haven Tea Rooms, cross a lane to resume towpath walking under the B4095 to another split-bridge. The Manor House stands nearby and the Crab Mill Inn lies just along the road to Henley.*

7. *Keep to the towpath for over a mile. At the second bridge, follow the drive of Preston Hill Farm to the right to reach Pettiford Lane. (Where the drive bends, look for an ancient moat on the right.)*

8. *Turn right over Pettiford Bridge to a stile/gate on the left. Cross to a little footbridge at the far right corner of a vast meadow and follow the River Alne upstream to Blackford Mill.*

Continued on page 82

9. *Bear left beside the mill and right at the end of it. Go over a railed bridge and follow a fenced path to a stile leading to Henley High School's playing fields. Cross to a stile on the A3400 and turn right into the town.*

Access by train and bus
Train to Henley in Arden (Birmingham Snow Hill–Stratford upon Avon line). Midland Red South Birmingham–Stratford upon Avon services.

Refreshments
The Crab Mill Inn and the Haven Tea Rooms at Preston Bagot; inns, cafes and ice-cream at Henley in Arden.

St John's Church, High Street, Henley in Arden

Warwick: Castle, Canal and Countryside

Outline

Warwick Race Course – Grand Union Canal – Hatton – Wedgnock
Old Park – Warwick

Summary

Easy walking across the Race Course and along the Grand Union Canal towpath to
Hatton, then on good tracks and bridleways to join a farm road with a distant
prospect of Warwick, before descending to the town.

Attractions

There is so much to see in Warwick that, if time is to be found for a ramble, a choice
has to be made. A good idea is to visit the Castle in the morning and to walk in the
afternoon. Allow over two hours for the Castle buildings, plus time for exploring
the grounds.

Warwick Castle grew over many centuries, beginning with the Mound raised in
914 by Ethelfleda, daughter of King Alfred, and achieving its present impressive
appearance in the late 18th century. In 1978 the Castle was sold by the Earl of
Warwick to Madame Tussaud's.

As a military fortress its defences were rarely put to the test, though in 1264,
during the Barons' War against Henry III, the north wall was smashed in and the
Earl and Countess captured, and in 1642 the Castle survived a two weeks' siege by
Royalists. A serious fire occurred in 1871, when the Private Apartments and Great
Hall were damaged.

We enter the Courtyard by the Gate House and find the Armoury to our left.
The weapons and suits of armour on display are fascinating, as are the battlements,
a walk along which involves climbing and descending some 200 steps.

Overlooking the River Avon are the Private Apartments and State Rooms, built
in sumptuous style during the 17th and 18th centuries. Madame Tussaud's has
peopled the Apartments with realistic wax figures representing a weekend party in
1898, when the guests included the Prince of Wales (later King Edward VII) and
young Winston Churchill.

The Dungeon and the Torture Chamber, though very interesting, are not to
everyone's taste, nor is the Watergate (or Ghost) Tower. A tape relates how Sir
Fulke Greville was murdered there by a manservant in 1628. He is said to haunt the
room to this day.

Warwick Racecourse is also known as Lammas Field. Lammas, the first day of
August, was formerly a harvest festival. Certain lands normally used for growing
crops were then opened for common pasture and other purposes.

The canal we follow was originally the Warwick & Birmingham. An information board at Hatton Bottom Lock outlines its history. Opened in 1800, it

Continued on page 86

Route 18

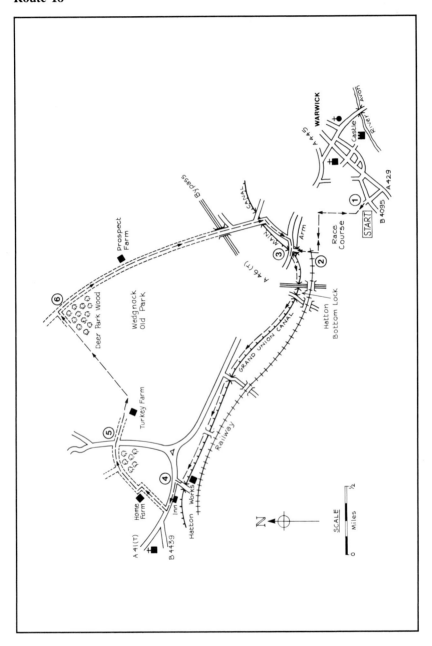

Route 18

Warwick: Castle, Canal and Countryside   6 miles

Start

*Free car-park at Warwick Race Course, off B4095 (OS Sheet 151 GR 277647).
Alternatively Saltisford Canal Trust car-park, off A425 (GR 271656), Hatton
Bottom Lock picnic area (GR 266655) or pay car-park at Hatton (GR 243669).*

Route

1. *From the public car-park within the main entrance of Warwick Race Course, go
through a gap in the course railings to a direction post and take the path that climbs
diagonally right towards two large oaks. Walk right of a line of trees to the north
side of the course and follow the outside of the white railings to the left.*

2. *At the turn, bear sharp right, leave the course by ducking under a fence at a corner,
climb a stile and ascend to the right to reach a stile above railway lines. Cross
carefully, follow a fenced path between factories and go over the Saltisford Arm of
the Grand Union Canal (passing the Saltisford Canal Trust car-park) to the A425
Birmingham Road.*

3. *Bear left over the main canal and descend, right, to the towpath. Follow it under the
bridge and soon under the Bypass – A46(T) – to Hatton Bottom Lock, and
continue for 1¾ miles to the car-park and British Waterways' Workshops at
Hatton.*

4. *Turn right to the A41(T) and left along its footpath. Pass the Waterman Inn and
bear right onto the surfaced drive of Home Farm. Turn left beside the outbuildings
and left again beyond them, then right through double-gates to a track running left
of woods. At a track junction fork right to a lane.*

5. *Go right for a few yards and take a track on the left to Turkey Farm. From a gate,
skirt left of the farm buildings and pass a pond to enter a sloping field. Turn left and
follow the bridleway alongside a hedge, first on the right of it, then on the left. Go
through a gate and take the track past Deer Park Wood to a metalled drive.*

6. *Turn right for ½ mile to Prospect Farm (the prospect is of Warwick, dominated by
the tall, slim tower of St Mary's Church) and, in another ½ mile or so, cross the A46
Bypass bridge. Just beyond, bear right at a junction and continue to the A425. Turn
right, then left over the Saltisford Arm of the canal, and retrace your steps back
across the Race Course to the car-park.*

amalgamated with others to form the Grand Union Canal Company in 1929. A great modernisation scheme begun in 1932 was never completed, because the government grant proved inadequate, but disused original locks can be seen beside their 1930s replacements at the Bottom Lock and at some of the other 21 locks that raise the canal 150 feet out of the Avon valley.

Towards the end of the walk we reach Prospect Farm in Wedgnock Old Park (now farmland) and enjoy a fine view of Warwick, crowned by the tower of the Collegiate Church of St Mary.

Refreshments
Inns and cafes in Warwick; restaurants and cafe at Castle; inn at Hatton; picnic site at Hatton Bottom Lock.

Access by train or bus
Train to Warwick (Birmingham–Leamington Spa line). Midland Red South services from Coventry, Kenilworth, Leamington Spa and Stratford upon Avon.

Ducks on the green at Radway

Wilmcote and the Stratford Canal

Outline

Wilmcote – Newnham – Stratford Canal – Wilmcote

Summary

An easy short walk over fields from the village of Wilmcote northwards to the hamlet of Newnham and back along the towpath of the Stratford-on-Avon Canal, a scenic waterway winding its way through pastoral countryside. The towpath walk can be extended for an indefinite distance either northwards towards Wootton Wawen from (4) or southwards from the bridge on the edge of Wilmcote to see the locks near Stratford.

Attractions

The village of Wilmcote is known the world over as the home of Mary Arden, William Shakespeare's mother. Her former house, now open to the public, is visited every year by thousands of literary pilgrims, anxious to soak up as many of the Bard's associations as possible.

Dating from the 16th century, the house is a beautiful half-timbered structure which, together with its associated farm buildings and the implements and artifacts they contain, provides us with a striking impression of what life was like in rural Warwickshire through bygone centuries up to the present day.

Newnham, reached over the fields along well-waymarked footpaths, is by contrast a quiet place today, but this was not always so. There were extensive quarries near the village in Tudor times, which supplied stone for the building of Clopton Bridge at Stratford-on-Avon and for the rebuilding of St Mary's Church at Warwick after its destruction by fire in 1694. Visiting Newnham today, it is hard to realise that it once had a population of over 300 people when its quarries were in their heyday.

The year 1816 was an important one for the people of Stratford and Wilmcote, for in that year the so-called Stratford-on-Avon Canal was opened. Although it had only a short life as a working waterway – it was bought by a railway company in 1856 – during this time it carried vast quantities of coal from the Midlands collieries, as well as stone from the local quarries.

Like so many canals, however, it was allowed to fall into ruin from the 1880s onwards and by 1945 the section covered on this walk was unusable. In the 1960s, a valiant effort was made to restore the canal for use as a recreational amenity and on July 11th 1964 the official re-opening was carried out by the Queen Mother.

Today the winding canal towpath makes a delightful walk, with flowers, birds and

Continued on page 90

Route 19

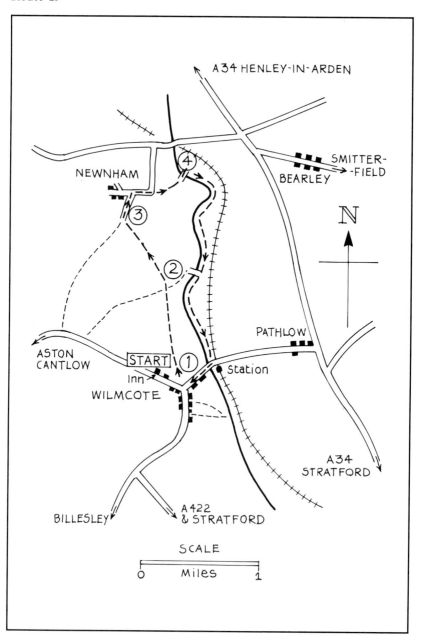

A34 HENLEY-IN-ARDEN

SMITTER-
-FIELD
BEARLEY

NEWNHAM

④

③

N

②

PATHLOW

ASTON
CANTLOW

START ①

Station

Inn
WILMCOTE

A34
STRATFORD

BILLESLEY

A422
& STRATFORD

SCALE

0   Miles   1

88

Route 19

Wilmcote and the Stratford Canal   3¾ miles

Start

Wilmcote village, 3 miles NW of Stratford-on-Avon. The village can be reached along minor roads from either the A422 or the A3400. Park as near as possible to the crossroads in the centre of the village, from which the walk begins. (O.S. Landranger Sheet 151, GR 164582).

Route

1. *Follow the direction indicated by the waymark sign (yellow arrow) opposite the Post Office. The public footpath passes behind Mary Arden's House, between a hedge and the boundary fence. Cross two stiles and follow the hedge on the right. After crossing two more stiles, the path, which is well marked by white arrows, keeps an intermittent tree-lined hedge on the left over a long field. Cross a bridleway (indicated by a blue arrow on a gate on the left), just beyond which the route veers to the left.*

2. *Keep on along this obvious line over 4 stiles, still with hedges on the left, before eventually crossing a small field to reach a grassy lane over a stile by a gate.*

3. *Turn right along the lane, passing Retreat Farm, to reach a road. The small village of Newnham lies to the left. The route continues to the right as far as a sharp left-hand bend. Leave the road here, taking the left-hand of two waymarked footpaths, i.e. over a stile by a gate. Cross a field to a stile in a paddock fence, leaving the paddock via another stile at the overgrown junction of two hedges. Go through the right-hand hedge and swing to the left, following the hedge on the left, before climbing right along the field edge for a short distance to reach the canal towpath over a metal bridge.*

4. *Turn right along the towpath and follow it the two miles or so back to the edge of Wilmcote, which is reached by climbing up to the road at the first concrete bridge and following the pavement to the right past Mary Arden's House to the crossroads and the start.*

insects to enjoy, together with quaint iron bridges spanning the 'cut' at intervals, split in the centre to allow tow-ropes to pass through.

Refreshments
Wilmcote − The Mason's Arms.

Mary Arden's House

Piper's Hill Common and Hanbury Park

Outline

Piper's Hill − Park Hill − Hanbury Hall − Hanbury Church − Piper's Hill

Summary

From the hilltop beechwood at Piper's Common you walk down into a valley to join a long, straight (muddy) track, obviously an old road. To your left are the green flanks of low hills. Soon after, you climb a bank and can walk the ridge of these hills, disclosing magnificent views. Next comes a couple of miles of undulating pasture leading to Hanbury Park, one of the National Trust's pocket statelies. Finally, perched on an isolated hill you meet Hanbury Church.

The long track we mentioned is a bridleway which usually makes it a welly walk. The rest of the walk is on grassland, very pleasant and easy.

If you do not want to do the main walk this time, we offer a short alternative which is a simple circuit of the woodland. This gives you views to the west which in summer might not be visible from the top.

Attractions

Piper's Hill Common is on a steep, sandstone outcrop about 350 feet high topped by a mature beech wood. It gives huge views over rural Worcestershire, pasture and ploughed land, woods and hedges misting away to distant hills. To the west are the humpbacked Abberley Hills and slightly north of them Shropshire's Clee Hills. South-west lie the craggier Malverns and, to the south, the big dome of Bredon Hill.

The woodland covers about 35 acres. There are some fine trunky old oaks, but it is largely beech. This is not common in the Midlands, and the only other predominantly beech woods are the small plantation on Frankley Beeches south of Birmingham, and on the crest of Adams Hill in the Clent Hills. All three are plantations rather than natural woodland, and this one was created by the Vernon family who owned nearby Hanbury Hall.

The walk takes you to the front gate of Hanbury Hall, a gorgeous, grand and sumptuous house, but to a very comfortable and domestic scale. Hanbury was completed in 1701 for Thomas Vernon, though the two little pavilions close to the footpath are Victorian. It is not certain who designed it.

St Mary's Church, Hanbury, stands on another sandstone hill, this one about 300 feet high. It has seen an Iron Age fort and a Saxon monastery, but the present church looks, from the outside, very four-square classically Georgian. In fact the tower was built in 1793. The interior is a surprising contrast, the only Georgian element being the handsome wooden gallery on slender piers. The nave is medieval with arcades of pointed arches, those on the south side dating from 1210. The chancel is Victorian, by G E Street who designed the London Law Courts. It is disappointingly ordinary apart from the glowing east window dominated by brilliant reds and blues.

Refreshments
There are acorns, berries and a few ponds at the start, and it makes a nice picnic place. Some people may prefer the pub at Hanbury, which is about 1¼ miles south on the main road. WARNING: Although the pub is only a short way from the south end of this walk, the connecting road is dangerous and not for children.

Public Transport
There is no bus service.

Piper's Hill Common

Piper's Hill Common

Route 20

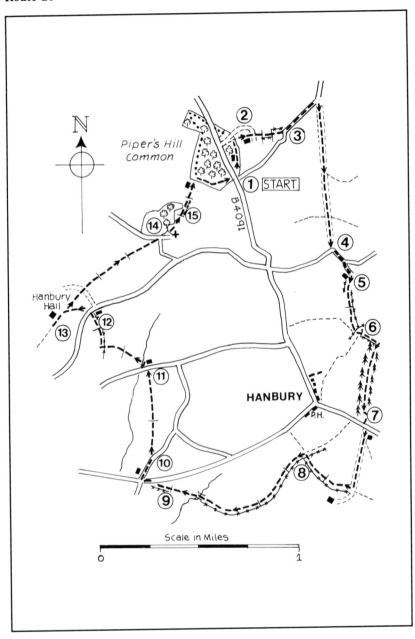

Route 20

Piper's Hill Common and Hanbury Park   6 miles

Start

Park on Piper's Hill. There are commonly used areas at the north (Bromsgrove) side, the south side and in the middle of the woods. This walk is described from the south side.

   Piper's Hill Common is the hilltop beechwood on the B4091 Bromsgrove to Hanbury road, about four miles south of Bromsgrove at map refrence SO 958648. Landranger Map 150 – Worcester and the Malverns.

   If you do not want to do the main walk, we can offer a short alternative. See the notes after the main walk. If you are vigorous you can do both.

Route

1. *From the car park on the south side of the wood, find the dirt track round the eastern edge. Follow it (with the woods on your left) past some houses and a thatched cottage right, to a gate and cattle grid right.*

2. *Cross the cattle grid and continue over the grass (NOT down the track), passing two trees on your left. Take the left of the two gates into the field AHEAD (not the yard). Walk with the fence on your right and take the gate, then with the hedge on your left to the corner stile and lane.*

3. *Walk ahead for about 400 yards to a left bend by a pond. Take the green track right for about ¾ mile, to meet the bend of a road.*

4. *Go ahead about 150 yards to the road junction, and take the right fork. Pass a cottage right and, immediately after, take the gate right. Walk with the hedge on your right to the field corner by a pond. Go through the hedge gap right to the next field.*

5. *Go left beside the hedge and cross the corner stile. Continue to the next corner and cross the stile left (NOT ahead). Cross the brick culvert and the next stile, then the twin stiles ahead.*

6. *Go up with the hedge on your right. Reach the crest and go to the far corner of the wood to cross the stile right. Go ahead along the left (upper) edge of the wood for about 700 yards. Meet a thicket and deep pit and take the stile left. Go right to the stile and road. (GREAT CARE – DO NOT CROSS HERE).*

7. *Go left up the verge to the 40mph sign, then cross the road and enter the gate on the right of the farm. Follow the concrete track to a hedge before a cattle grid. Turn right and walk with the hedge on your left (past a stile left and over a stile) over the crest, and down to take the left of two gates.*

8. *Go left with the hedge on your left for about ½ mile (via two stiles and past a stile left), to cross a wooden footbridge. Go ahead and cross the stile. Bear half left to pass the midfield pond and trees close on your left, and take the gate beyond.*

9. *Go ahead, bearing right to take the mid-hedge stile by the gate, and reach the B4090. Go left to the crossroads and take the lane right. Walk about 200 yards to just past the power lines and take the stile left.*

10. *Turn half right. Note ahead a red brick house and two black and white. Head for the middle (b & w) house, via a mid-fence stile, and take the gate on its right on to a lane.*

11. *Go left 20 yards and at the end of the garden take the gate right. Go ahead to the projecting hedge corner and cross the stream. Go right a few paces to the power pole. Look right of the power lines to the red house and head for its left side to take a gate. Go to the far right field corner and cross the stile. Go ahead a few paces, cross the stile right and continue to a gate and lane.*

12. *Enter the hedge gap opposite and cross the stile. Bear half left to pass the midfield pines and take the gate/stile. Go ahead a few yards to see the front of Hanbury Hall.*

13. *TURN BACK, pass through the previous gate/stile and go ahead, to pass the trees and pond close on your left. Keep this line over the drive and past the oaks to take the gate/stile left into the avenue of trees. Follow the avenue, then a field path to the kissing gate and lane.*

14. *Go right a few paces to the bend and take the lane left up to the church. Enter the churchyard, pass the tower on your right, then bear left to take the kissing gate. Follow the diagonal field path down to take a kissing gate.*

15. *Go right along the hedge to the kissing gate and track. Go ahead, pass the mighty oak, a house left and a path left, and go on 40 yards to a right bend.*
    EITHER take the steep earth path ahead to the top. Go right through the woods to find the road and your car park.
    OR continue up the track to the road and go up left to the start.

Short Alternative
(a) *Follow Para 1 of the main walk, but at the cattle grid continue on the wood edge track (becomes a path) to the B4091.*
(b) *Cross and continue on the wood edge path to a small green with houses left. Turn sharp left and return into the wood, following paths along the wood's western edge, past houses right, to the far corner where you meet a track, a house right, and a mighty oak.*
(c) *Go left 40 yards to a right bend, then take EITHER of the alternatives in main walk Para 15.*

Hanbury Church

The Worcester and Birmingham Canal

Outline
Tardebigge Church − Queen's Head Inn, Stoke Pound − Dusthouse Lane − Grimley Lane − Tardebigge Church

Summary
Walking along canal towpaths is both easy and full of interest. The leisurely tempo, too, has its own special appeal − so much so that I suspect that many walkers will be content to retrace their steps from the Queen's Head, rather than part company with the towpath for the return route. Those who do 'complete the course' should enjoy the short diversion from the canal, however, especially any railway enthusiasts. In any case, the last stage of the walk entails retracing the route from the reservoir to Tardebigge Church.

Attractions
Few hamlets can boast such a proud claim to fame as tiny Tardebigge. St Bartholomew's Church, perched on its hill, was built in 1777 and its 135-foot spire is a landmark for miles around. Together with the nearby school and rectory, it makes an attractive group. But it was some 40 years after the church was built that Tardebigge's name became famous. In 1815, the Worcester to Birmingham canal was finally opened after a quarter of a century of difficult construction, including the building of the huge flight of locks we see today. These locks carry the waterway over 200 feet up the hillside in 2½ miles to the mouth of the Tardebigge Tunnel and were constructed by gangs of navvies who moved thousands of tons of earth with their spades and wheelbarrows.

Today the canal is still in use, although the trading narrow boats of bygone times have been replaced by pleasure craft.

Two features connected with the supply of water for this stretch of the canal are of special interest. One is the former pumping station, which after lying derelict for many years has now been converted into a restaurant. The other is Tardebigge Reservoir, built to supply water to replace that lost by the constant opening and closing of the lock gates.

This reservoir is now a haven for wildlife, especially birds, and enthusiasts should come equipped with binoculars. Among the species present throughout the year are mallard, coot, moorhen, great crested grebe and Canada goose, all of which feed in the reedy margins of the reservoir.

For those deciding to complete the full route, the stretch of walking away from the canal is over footpaths and along minor roads, and provides a glimpse of the pleasant countryside through which the great feat of canal engineering was constructed.

Refreshments
Stoke Pound — The Queen's Head: Restaurant, children welcome.

Lock near Tardebigge

Route 21

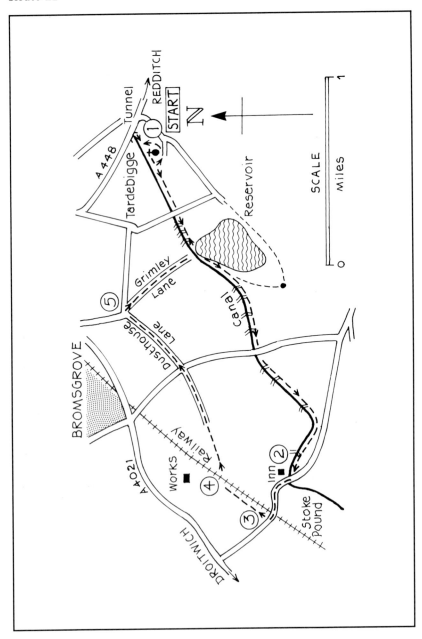

100

Route 21

The Worcester and Birmingham Canal   6 miles

Start

Tardebigge Church. This prominent landmark stands ¼ mile south of the A418, midway between Bromsgrove and Redditch. (OS Landranger Sheet 139, GR 996692). Park near the church.

Route

1. *At the entrance to the churchyard, turn right through a kissing gate and follow the path down to the canal. After seeing the mouth of the Tardebigge Tunnel, turn left along the towpath. The route follows the towpath for about 2½ miles as far as the bridge by the Queen's Head Inn.*

2. *From the bridge (or the inn), turn right along the road to pass a nursery (on the left) and a pumping station ön the right.ˆ Keep straight on as far as a railway bridge.*

3. *Immediately beyond the bridge, climb up the grassy bank on the right to reach a metalled path running straight alongside the railway. Follow this path until it bends to the left.*

4. *Climb the steps on the right (yellow arrow) and cross this busy main line track with great care. In the field, turn left to follow the edge parallel to the railway. At the end of the field, bear right along the hedge to a wide opening. Turn through this gap, keeping to the right of a hedge, and proceed through a gate and into a lane. Keep straight on along this lane, passing a road signposted to Upper Bentley on the right, and keep on to another junction, with Walnut Lane on the left and Grimley Lane on the right.*

5. *Turn right up Grimley Lane, passing the entrance to Grimley Hall drive. From the summit, the land dips down to the canal. Cross the bridge to rejoin the towpath alongside Tardebigge Reservoir and turn left to retrace steps back towards Tardebigge Church, which can be reached from the towpath by a signposted path alongside the lock-keeper's cottage by Tardebigge Top Lock.*

Salwarpe Valley and Droitwich Canal

Outline
Salwarpe village – Droitwich Canal – Mildenham Mill –
Bowling Green Inn – Salwarpe village

Summary
In contrast to Route 21, the greater part of which is along the towpath of a working canal, this walk is routed for about half of its length along a disused waterway. Instead of the lively and colourful sight of narrow boats and other vessels negotiating the locks, the walk traces what remains of a long-abandoned trade route and ends with a stretch of pleasant, easy walking on minor roads and footpaths in the attractive Salwarpe Valley.

Attractions
Derelict canals have their own distinctive appeal. Their original attractions – brightly-painted boats, well-maintained lock gates, tidy towpaths – have long since gone, but years of neglect have given them a new kind of fascination that many historians, naturalists, ramblers—and families, too – find irresistible.

The Droitwich Canal opened in 1771 and was constructed to develop the salt trade, for which the town of Droitwich had been famous for centuries. Its building was supervised by James Brindley, the celebrated self-taught engineer who had been responsible for the first great navigation, as canals were then called, in Lancashire. Its length was short – only 6¾ miles – but as the first efficient trade link between Droitwich, Bristol (via the River Severn) and later Birmingham (via the Worcester and Birmingham canal), it was a busy and prosperous waterway until growing competition from the railways finally led to its abandonment just before the Second World War.

Like many other derelict canals, this one has attracted the attention of enthusiasts bent on restoring it to its original navigable state. There is evidence of their efforts early on the walk in the form of new lock gates with a recently renovated lock-keeper's cottage alongside.

Children may well prefer discovering traces of the canal's history, rather than admiring the restorers' efforts, however, and there is plenty of evidence for the young industrial archaeologist to search for. Close inspection of the locks (easier than on a working canal) reveals overflow openings and ground paddles, while nearby can be seen lengths of old narrow-gauge rail and rusting side-tipping trucks.

Naturalists in the family, meanwhile, will be fully absorbed in studying the wildlife that has colonised this disused waterway. Water-loving plants, such as reeds, reedmace and great willowherb grow abundantly along damp stretches, while teazel, burdock, St John's wort, bartsia, and a host of other wild flowers splash their colourful mantle along the overgrown margins elsewhere.

From May to August, skulking little sedge warblers rattle out their song from this dense cover. Moorhens and mallard breed in the safety of the low vegetation, whilst sharp-eyed spotters missing out on seeing a kingfisher by the canal can still make amends by catching a fleeting glimpse of this splendid bird skimming along the nearby river Salwarpe, as I was fortunate enough to do one August afternoon.

Nearby Attractions
Hawford dovecote, 3 miles SW of Salwarpe (National Trust).

Refreshments
Hadley Bowling Green Inn: Snacks and lunches, garden, children welcome.

Lock Keeper's House, Salwarpe

Route 22

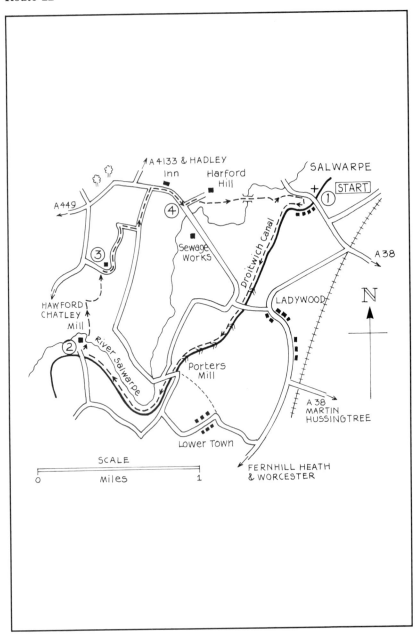

SALWARPE

A4133 & HADLEY
Inn
Harford
Hill

START

A449

4

A38

3

Droitwich Canal

Sewage
Works

N

LADYWOOD

HAWFORD
CHATLEY
Mill

River Salwarpe

2

Porters
Mill

A38
MARTIN
HUSSINGTREE

SCALE

Lower Town

FERNHILL HEATH
& WORCESTER

0   Miles   1

Route 22

Salwarpe Valley and Droitwich Canal   4½ miles

Start

Salwarpe village, approximately 1 mile south-west of Droitwich. Approached by

minor road from A38, ¼ mile south of the junction with the B4090. Park by the church. (OS Landranger Sheet 150, GR 875621).

Route

1. *Walk past the church along the lane and, at a signpost, cross over a stile on the left to follow a footpath. In 40 metres cross another stile, also on the left. Climb the bank to the canal towpath and turn right. In about a mile, after passing a lock, cross a road by a bridge and return to the towpath. At the next road, turn left parallel to the canal and soon, at a T-junction, turn left to rejoin the towpath. Another mile or so of towpath walking follows to the next bridge, where the walk leaves the canal at Mildenham Mill.*

2. *Immediately before the bridge and the gateway to the mill, turn sharp right through a metal gate to follow a footpath parallel to the canal towpath. This path, which can be muddy, bends to the left to cross a metal bridge. Over the bridge, bear left and head for the first of two metal handgates at each end of another bridge. Climb the bank ahead to pass through a gate (fitted with a special catch for horse riders) and keep straight on. Soon the path swings to the right with a pylon ahead. At a T-junction of paths, turn left and keep straight on to meet a road.*

3. *About a mile of minor road walking now follows. Turn right and pass a black and white farmhouse. At a junction by Woodbury Cottage, turn left to reach a T-junction. Turn right (Ladywood on signpost). The Hadley Bowling Green Inn is soon reached on the left. From the inn, keep on in the same direction as before and, at the foot of the slope, watch for a footpath signposted "Salwarpe ¾" on the left.*

4. *Follow this path along the track until another signpost indicates a deviation to the right. This entails dipping down the bank to a barbed wire fence and keeping this on the right as far as a stile. (This section of the walk can be somewhat overgrown in summer). Cross the stile and climb the bank ahead. Salwarpe Church comes into view at the top. Aim for the church tower, crossing the River Salwarpe by a metal bridge. Keep straight on with a fence on the left. Follow the fence round to the right to a stile at the corner of the field. Climb and descend a bank, following the yellow arrows, before passing the second stile (to the canal) crossed earlier, to reach the lane to the church by the first stile encountered at the start of the walk.*

Chaddesley Corbett and the Woods

Outline

Chaddesley Corbett — Chaddesley Wood — Woodcote Green — High Wood —
Nutnells Wood — Chaddesley Wood — Chaddesley Corbett

Summary

From the delightful village of Chaddesley Corbett you climb easily over fields to a
range of small hills crowned with one of the few remnants of the ancient forest of
Feckenham. The highest point is only about 130 metres above sea level, but they
command fair views, given that the village and the surrounding plain lie at about 75
metres.

Most of the walk is in woodland with a great variety of trees. Watch out for fallow
and muntjac deer. At the beginning and end are fields, usually arable, but in the
middle is a green, pastoral interlude. Here you pass a house where they sell walking
sticks and whistles made from local trees.

The field sections may be muddy in wet weather, but the only first class, hippo-
wallow certified, guaranteed mud is in Nutnells Wood. Happily for non-hippos, little
paths have developed which skirt some of the deepest.

Attractions

Chaddesley Corbett is one of the most delightful villages in the Midlands. Flint tools
from between 2,000 and 5,000 BC have been unearthed at a burial mound to the north-
east. The Roman road from Droitwich to Greensforge west of Dudley passed close
by and there is some evidence of a Roman settlement. But the first real evidence of
a village is from a charter of 816 granting land including the village to the Bishop of
Worcester. The general outline of the village seems to have been planned in the 12th
century by the then Lords of the Manor, the Corbett family. Down the following
centuries it was the centre of an agricultural landscape. There were saddlers, smiths,
carpenters, masons and butchers, and markets were held in the main street. Although
there was an important rural metal industry making knife and scythe blades at the
nearby villages of Drayton and Harvington, Chaddesley never grew into a town and
the houses and plots of land along the main street hardly differ from maps of 1697
and 1745. The result of these quiet centuries is a main street with buildings from all
periods, timber framing from the 15th to the 17th centuries, and brick from the 18th
and 19th. The houses and shops are of all heights, with gables and dormers, bays,
bows, porches and arches, yet with no conscious planning at all, the whole street is
totally harmonious. Get the leaflet from the church which describes each building.

Entering the churchyard of St Cassian's you notice first the tower and spire, but
the glory of it is the chancel. The Victorian stained glass in the east window is quite
nice standard stuff, but look at the stonework. The clear windows of the nave flood
it with light and the bare stone walls help to enhance the chancel. The earliest visible

work in the church is in the nave, those mighty, round Norman arches from about 1150. The font is from the same period, with a Celtic knot-like pattern round rim and base, and dragons' tails writhing exuberantly round the bowl. Look also for the memorial to Humphrey Pakington, a one time Lord of the Manor. He may have died in 1631, but this is a memorial no-one will forget. We have black marble, white marble, a family crest neatly wedged into a broken pediment and curly alabaster things. Get the leaflets and make sure you leave lots of money.

In medieval times the Forest of Feckenham was a Royal Hunting Forest and covered the area between Worcester and the Clent Hills, and east from the River Severn to the edges of Warwickshire. Today there are just six fragmentary groups of woods, the largest of which is the Chaddesley Woods group. The woodlands reflect the seductive, hilly contours of north Worcestershire with summits of 125, 137 and 200 metres. This and the nature of the soil suggest why they survived the rest of the Forest. Medieval farmers would naturally clear and farm first the level and fertile land, and these hills are neither. Although there is a fair proportion of conifers, at least half the woodland is native broadleaved trees with wonderful airy oakwoods. High Wood, which you visit on this walk, is a fairyland for bluebells. Look out for the pretty chestnut and white spotted fallow deer and the tiny muntjac, a reclusive species no bigger than a dog which can hide in a small bramble patch.

Attractions
The Swan and The Talbot are attractive and well known for their food and drink. Especially the drink, since they serve Batham's and Banks's beer respectively.

Public Transport
Buses run occasionally between Kidderminster and Bromsgrove. Enquiries − 01345 125436.

Route 23

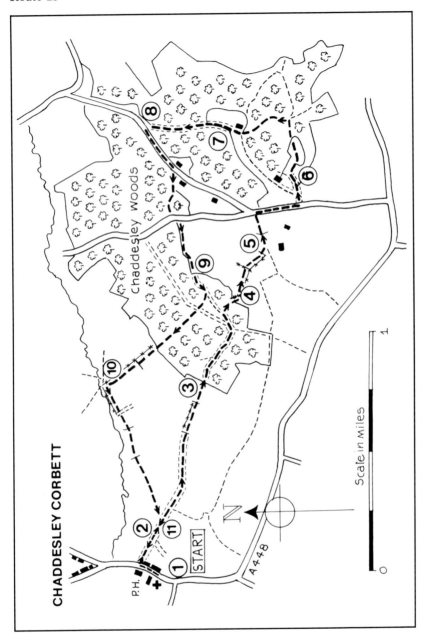

108

Route 23

Chaddesley Corbett and the Woods   5 miles

Start

Park in the main street of Chaddesley Corbett near the church at SO 892736. OS Landranger Map 139 – Birmingham.

Chaddesley Corbett lies on the A448 Kidderminster-Bromsgrove road, which is the easiest approach. However, you can reach Chaddesley from the north through a network of lanes south of Belbroughton, which is just south of the A491 Bromsgrove-Stourbridge road.

Route

1. *From the church walk up the main street to The Swan and take the footpath opposite (right). Pass the end of a street left and follow the power lines to cross a stile on to the bend of a track.*

2. *Follow the track ahead for about 500 yards until it bends sharp left. Go AHEAD with the hedge on your left and cross the field corner stile. Go ahead passing just left of the lowest part of the power lines (via a stile) and cross a stile into the woods.*

3. *Follow the path ahead to meet a track. Go right, rising steeply to a T-junction of tracks. Go left past a track left, then on about 100 yards to take a small path right. Follow it down to the wood edge and cross the stile.*

4. *Turn half left, cross the field corner to the projecting hedge corner and take a stile. Walk with the hedge on your right to take a stile right, by the gate. Walk with the hedge on your right, bearing left to a gate about 80 yards left of the right field corner. Cross the stile.*

5. *Cross the next stile ahead, then go left (via stiles) to cross a stile 15 yards left of the gate. on to a lane. Go right about 330 yards and take the track left. Walk about 100 yards (past a gate) and enter the drive right ("White Lodge"). Round the left bend and approach the house, but turn right through the gap between buildings to cross the stile.*

6. *Go right up the EDGE OF THE WOOD, through a fence gap (or gate) to the crest, then curve left with the wood to join a fence on the left. Follow this to cross a stile. Follow the woodland path to a path junction. Go left, pass two paths right and go over the crest, then down towards the cottage and cross a stile (? bust) on to the corner of a track.*

7. *Go right and pass the cottage, then via kissing gates and a clear (muddy) woodland*

path to take a kissing gate on to a lane. Go left for about 300 yards and take a track right marked "Randan", opposite the house "Eventide".

8. Follow the drive to the garage, take the path on its right and cross a stile. Follow the wood edge path (via stiles) to a lane. Cross the stile opposite and walk with the wood on your right. Cross a fence, then rise over the crest and take a stile right into the wood.

9. Go left about 200 yards to meet a wide, green path right. Turn right on the green path, walk over the crest, and down to take the wood edge stile. Go down with the hedge on your right for two fields, past the pylon, to the stile right. DON'T CROSS IT.

10. Turn left and walk parallel with the right hedge to cross two stiles and a track. Bear slightly left to take the mid-hedge stile. Go ahead, aiming just left of the church steeple to the last low building, and go through the hedge gap on to a track.

11. Go right to the left bend and take the stile ahead. Follow the path back to the village.

High Wood

Romsley and Uffmoor Wood

Outline
Uffmoor Wood − St Kenelm's Church − Adams Hill − Walton Hill −
Romsley − Uffmoor Wood

Summary
After a short walk through Uffmoor Wood comes a very pretty stroll along a narrow
strip of woodland rising to St Kenelm's church. Then you climb more steeply over
grazing fields to the main car park for Adams Hill. You can find a steep path to the
top, or go with the crowd and follow the wheelchair route to near the summit. From
here there are some of the widest and best views in the Midlands.

Walking down Adams Hill you can decide whether to follow the very quiet lane
which follows for just over half a mile, or make up for cheating on Adams Hill by
climbing the much steeper Walton Hill.

From here the walk is fairly level, with a mixture of arable and grassland to
Romsley. The return route to Uffmoor Wood is all grassland with some nice ponds,
and much of it along the edge of Uffmoor Wood.

Attractions
Uffmoor Wood at the foot of the Clent Hills was one of the "Harris Brush" woods.
The famous Bromsgrove firm of paint brush makers once owned some 2,000 acres
of woodland in Worcestershire to supply themselves with brush handles. In the early
1980s they began to sell the woods one by one. A valuable group were bought by the
Worcestershire Nature Conservation Trust and this one by Woodland Trust. Wander
about as you wish; the Trusts allow free access.

Uffmoor has probably been woodland continuously since the last Ice Age, and
older trees include the uncommon whitebeam, bay willow and alder buckthorn. But
most of the present trees are young. Harris's planted larch, Scots pine, sycamore,
alder, ash and poplar to grow small roundwood for brush making, rather than
managing them to maturity to produce sawmill timber. This has created an unusual
and valuable habitat for wildlife.

St Kenelm's, its legend and its well were once the centre of a thriving village of
Kenelmstowe. Kenelm (the story says) was the infant son of King Kenulph of Mercia
who died in 821. He was succeeded by his brother Ceolwulf, but unfortunately
somebody had crowned young Kenelm, Ceolwulf had the lad taken to a royal hunting
lodge on the Clent Hills, where a rascal called Askobert slunk up behind him with
an axe (what do you expect of someone called Askobert?) and chopped off the little
chap's head.

Meanwhile, back in Rome, the Pope was interrupted during Mass when a dove
whizzed into the basilica carrying a scroll written in Anglo-Saxon. Conveniently, the
place was packed with Anglo-Saxon priests, who translated the thing into Latin. "Lo,

in a mead of kine, under a thorn; Of head bereft, lieth poor Kenelm, king-born''. Enquiries led to the cow field of an old woman. One of her beasts seemed to eat nothing, but grew fatter and meatier than the rest, and lo, the spot where it was wont to graze revealed the chopped-up bits of young Kenelm, plus a jolly suspicious-looking axe. Naturally, when they bustled off to bury him, a spring of pure water sprang forth which would cure more ailments than Lily the Pink's rather later Medicinal Compound. It became a place of pilgrimage and the village of Kenelmstowe made a good thing of it.

The church was built over the spring, which used to emerge in an undercroft below the east end. It has now been diverted to a rather weedy spot at the bottom of a hollow to the north-east, which you pass on the walk. This is a very attractive small church with a charming rural calm. The nave and chancel are Norman in red sandstone, the tower and buttresses are grey and date from the late 1400s. The porch in small, rosy red bricks is Tudor. The stonework is terribly weathered. The gargoyles may have been carved as the usual range of cartoon faces, but are now eaten away and quite ghastly. Four crocketed corner pinnacles have been replaced and by comparison look coarse and mechanical. Get the booklet from the church.

The Clent range includes two obvious hills, Walton at 315 metres to the east and Adams Hill to the west at 304 metres. But walk south from the summit of Walton Hill and you discover that it is a triangular massif with a long ridge running south to Calcutt Hill at 240 metres. They are part of a chain of high ground running across the southern edge of the West Midlands conurbation. In the far west is Kinver Edge, then come the Clent Hills. Further west and reaching 250 metres are the Waseley Hills, leading to the Lickey Hills at 285 metres. These are steep, miniature mountains with woods and bracken on the slopes and heather and bilberry on the crests. The north flank of Walton is the steepest part of the Clent Hills, but it is a big dome and views are limited. Adams Hill presents the furthest, finest views in the Midlands. In clear weather you can see to the north-west Shropshire's Wrekin, to the west are Brown Clee and Titterstone Clee, then, at a great distance, the Radnor Forest and Hay Bluff in the Black Mountains of mid-Wales. Worcestershire's Abberley Hills can usually be seen and the craggy Alp-like Malverns. To the south are Bredon Hill and Edge Hill in Warwickshire.

Romsley is a curious village. It has two rather nice pubs, a Post Office and a couple of shops, an interesting looking antique shop and a school, but there are no very old buildings and it has no centre. Most of the houses are modern. The strange fact that St Kenelm's is Romsley's parish church is a clue to its character. The village of Kenelmstowe mentioned above declined after the Reformation when pilgrimage ceased. But in the early 1800s a turnpike road was built between Bromsgrove and Dudley and so Romsley developed here. It is within easy reach of Bromsgrove and the West Midlands, but in a relaxed rural setting, and so became an attractive commuter dormitory.

Refreshments

Tea, coffee and snacks can be had at the car park on Adams Hill, and in summer there are usually mobile snack bars and things at the base of Walton Hill. There are two pubs in Romsley.

Public Transport

Buses run on the A456 between Birmingham, Halesowen and Stourbridge. Enquiries – 01905 766802.

St Kenelm's Church

113

Route 24

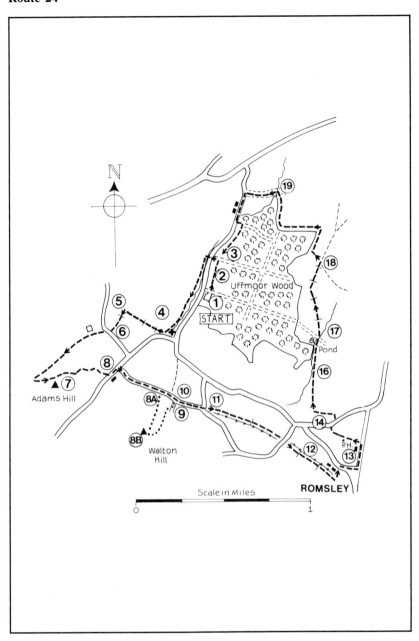

Route 24

Romsley and Uffmoor Wood   5 miles

Start

Start from the Woodland Trust's car park at map reference SO 947811, OS Landranger Map 139 − Birmingham. This lies on a lane running south from the A456 Birmingham-Kidderminster road, just east of the roundabout at Hayley Green, Halesowen.

Route

1. *From the car park return to the entrance track. Take the gap on the left side as you entered.*

2. *Follow the woodland path, parallel with the lane, to a wide track with a gate left and a white gate beyond.*

3. *Turn left through the gate and cross the lane to enter the drive opposite. Take the left of two gates and turn immediately left on a small fenced path. Follow a clear woodland path (later a field edge path) parallel with the stream left (via stiles) to the church.*

4. *From the church tower walk up to the lamp post. Go on four paces, then turn right on a faint path between the graves. Walk through a hedge gap and cross a small field to take the stile. Bear left and pass through the gappy hedge by the marked post. Continue the same line to the far left field corner and cross the stile.*

5. *Bear left to the marked post, then go with the hedge on your right past the 2nd post to the 3rd. Turn LEFT and cross the field corner stile. Go UP to the crest, heading for the left end of the line of tall trees, and cross a stile on to a lane.*

6. *Go right a few paces to enter the car park. You can go ahead to pass the loos, etc, on your right and follow the wheelchair route, or find one of the other paths to the summit, where there are four standing stones and a concrete trig point.*

7. *Stand with the trig point on your RIGHT and the four stones behind it. (Your back is to the main views). Walk ahead on the broad track for about 200 yards and take the path right by the fir cone sign (North Worcestershire Path). Follow the signs down to a lane.*

8. *Go left up to the junction and turn right. Walk about ¼ mile to the car park on the right.*

OPTION: To climb Walton Hill

8a. *Enter the car park and follow paths to the summit trig point.*

8b. *Stand at the trig point with your back to the little pine wood and walk forward 25 paces to a path. Follow the path down to a lane. Go left to the junction and turn right.*
   GO TO PARAGRAPH 10

9. *Continue on the lane for about 200 yards to a left fork and right bend. Go left.*

10. *Follow the lane for about 250 yards to the next fork. Go left a few paces and take the path at the left side of the fenced farm buildings.*

11. *Walk with the hedge on your right (via stiles) to a lane. Go left 15 paces and cross the stile right. Walk with the hedge on your left (through three fields) and through a thicket.*

12. *Now keep parallel with the left hedge; the path meanders. Pass the pit left, then bear left to a hedge corner and fork in the path. Go left down to the road.*

13. *Go right to the main road. Go left 250 yards to the school, right. Take the path opposite and follow it over several roads (at one point following the pavement ahead) to emerge at a lane.*

14. *Go left and take a stile right into the car park. Follow the stone path to the pavilion. Just BEFORE the building turn left and take the corner stile.*

15. *Follow the hedge to the corner, then turn right. Walk with the hedge on your left nearly ½ mile (via gates and stiles) to enter a woodland path ending at a stile to a field.*

16. *Go with the wood on your left, bearing a little right to pass the pond and take a stile at its end. Walk left across the head of the pond for 20 yards, then turn half right.*

17. *Follow the yellow topped posts for nearly ½ mile. (Where the posts seem to vanish, go ahead to see the next in a dip). When you come to a stile with a second stile just ahead, cross both stiles.*

18. *Turn left to the edge of the wood, then turn right. Walk with the wood on your left, round several corners, for about ½ mile to a stile and track by a brick bridge.*

19. *Follow the track left to the lane. Go left, pass a farm and a cottage right, and enter the wood left by the first gate.*

20. *Walk through the wood as you please. The direct route to your car park is on paths parallel with the lane.*

Abberley Hill

Outline

Wynniates Way − Abberley Hill − Hundred House Hotel − Abberley Hall −
Wynniates Way (optional: Abberley Village)

Summary

The wooded hills of Worcestershire make delightful walking for family parties. While
never exactly precipitous, these hill-walks nevertheless give children a sense of
achievement and provide adults with rewarding views of a countryside whose subtle
charms are far too often overlooked. The ascent to the 930-foot summit of Abberley
Hill is tackled at the beginning of this walk, when everybody is fresh, and although
the terrain remains undulating throughout, it is reassuring to know that the hardest
section of the route has been left behind!

Attractions

The scramble up to the concrete triangulation pillar near the start of the walk may well
prompt children to want to know something of the way in which the Ordnance Survey
puts our countryside on the map. Given clear visibility, they will begin to understand
why this hilltop vantage point was chosen as a survey site, for the view is extensive.

Prominent to the south-west is the clock tower known as Jones' Folly, erected just
over a century ago by the eccentric squire of Abberley for the sole purpose, according
to local belief, of looking down on his wealthy and influential neighbour at nearby
Great Witley Court! Away to the south rises Woodbury Hill, upon which Iron Age
people constructed a hill fort and where, in 1402, the Welsh leader Owen Glendower
encamped with his army during his campaign against King Henry IV. Over two
centuries later, Woodbury yet again provided the lofty setting for a minor historical
event. In 1645, an armed gathering of Worcestershire people—farmers, tradesmen and
ordinary villagers − declared their contempt and defiance of the armies − both Royalist
and Roundhead − that had robbed, bullied and terrorised them throughout the Civil
War − a bold new assertion of the old saying "A plague on both your houses!".

Historical associations are thick on the ground in this corner of Worcestershire.
As its distinctive sign suggests, the Georgian Hundred House Hotel boasts an out-of-
the-ordinary past, having once served as a coroner's court − surely one for the record
books.

Like the other woodland walks in this book, this one provides plenty of interest
for nature lovers. Whatever the time of year, tree-feeding and nesting birds can be
studied at close quarters. These include such small species as tits and treecreepers and
larger birds such as jays and woodpeckers. Woodland flowers add their share of
interest, while in autumn fungi of many kinds thrive on decaying wood.

Continued on page 120

117

Route 25

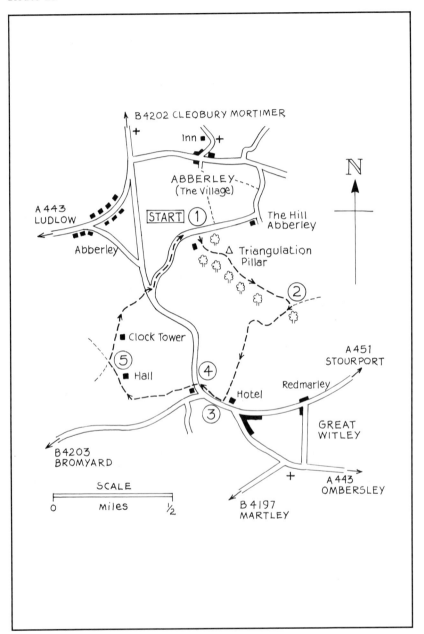

Route 25

Abberley Hill

2½ miles (plus optional 1¼ mile circular to Abberley village)

Start

Wynniates Way, a minor road climbing northwards from the A443, just to the east of its junction with the B4202, and a mile north-west of Great Witley. Limited parking on the verge just beyond the brow of the hill. (OS Landranger Sheet 150, GR 750674).

Route

1. *Walk back to the brow of the hill and cross the stile signposted "Worcestershire Way Main Route − North" on the left. The path climbs through woodland, following the waymark yellow arrows to reach a triangulation pillar at 930 feet above sea level. From the pillar keep on along the ridge with a metal fence on the right. The path narrows after the fence ends, but keep on straight ahead as far as a post showing the Worcestershire Way dipping to the left.*

2. *Leave the Way here, keeping straight on through the woods. Eventually the ground levels out, the path bears to the right, passes a manhole cover near a patch of marshy ground, skirts a fallen tree and dips left at a T-junction to leave the woodland at a stile. Cross a field, keeping a fence on the left. (There is a good view of the clock tower on the right). Cross another stile about 20 metres down from the corner. In the next field, keep the hedge on the left to meet a road (A443) at the Hundred House Hotel.*

3. *From the hotel, turn right along the A443. 50 metres past its junction with the B4203 cross the road to reach the entrance to a track to the right of a white cottage.*

4. *Follow this track, keeping left at a fork by a small pool on the right. The track winds uphill through woodland, passing a walled garden on the left, to a T-junction. Turn right, climbing through parkland to reach Abberley Hall (now a school). Follow the track around the buildings to reach a junction of 5 ways.*

5. *Follow the Worcestershire Way sign straight ahead. Pass a deer farm on the left and the clock tower behind the trees on the right and descend to a road (A443). Cross with care and walk up Wynniates Way, directly opposite, back to the car.*

Extending the route

Those families wishing to visit Abberley Village (as distinct from Abberley) to see the tiny restored Norman church of St Michael can do so by following the roads and footpaths (dotted lines) shown on the sketch map.

Nearby Attractions

Great Witley Court and Church: The former a ruin, having been burnt down in 1937, the latter a striking example of 18th century baroque architecture within an uninspiring exterior often likened to a warehouse!

Refreshments

Great Witley – Hundred House Hotel: Snacks and lunches, restaurant, children welcome.

Public Transport

An infrequent service links Great Witley with Worcester (Midland Red West).

The Hundred House Hotel, Great Witley

Wyre Forest

Outline

Far Forest − Callow Hill − Forest walk − Dowles Brook ford −
Wimperhill Wood − Far Forest

Summary

The Wyre Forest is a fascinating remnant of one of the vast tracts of wildwood that
once covered much of Midland England. Many families discover something of its
delights as a result of a visit to the Forestry Commission's centre at Callow Bank. For
those who prefer to 'go it alone', rather than keep to the well-trodden paths, there are
plenty of tempting alternatives, as this varied and fairly straightforward route shows.

Attractions

The very word 'forest' conjures up a host of romantic impressions in young and not-
so-young alike. Indeed, the name of the somewhat unremarkable village of Far Forest,
near which this walk begins, appealed so much to the region's novelist, Francis Brett
Young, that he used it as the title of one of his works. Although what remains of the
forest is dissected by roads and encroached upon by villages and scattered farms and
houses, it retains much of its atmosphere of remoteness and mystery. In fact, with the
abandoning of its coal and iron workings and the closure of the railway which once
passed through it, the forest seems to have closed in and returned to its former pre-
industrial state.

The Dowles Brook provides the forest with much of its charm. Fed by its tributary
streams, the Baveney and Man brooks, the Dowles Brook flows eastwards through
the trees to meet the Severn near Bewdley. It is said that its name means dark, or black
even, but this description bears little relation to the water, the purity of which attracts
three of our most colourful water-birds − the grey wagtail, the dipper and the
kingfisher.

The ford across the Dowles Brook (4 on the Map) is an ideal spot for children to
paddle and enjoy water-play.

In addition to water-birds, a wide range of woodland species are present, including
tits (blue, great, coal, long-tailed and marsh), goldcrests, treecreepers and
woodpeckers. Keen eyes will detect deer-prints in the mud. The insect population −
dragonflies, butterflies, moths and beetles—is extensive, while wood ants scuttle
backwards and forwards, carrying twigs far larger than themselves to further extend
nests already a metre or so high.

Last, but by no means least, the forest trees deserve special mention. Many are
very old − one gnarled and ancient oak is said to have a girth measuring 23½ feet.
The native hardwoods − oak, beech, birch, ash, hazel − are supplemented by more
recent plantings of softwood conifers, including larch, spruce and Douglas fir,

Continued on page 124

Route 26

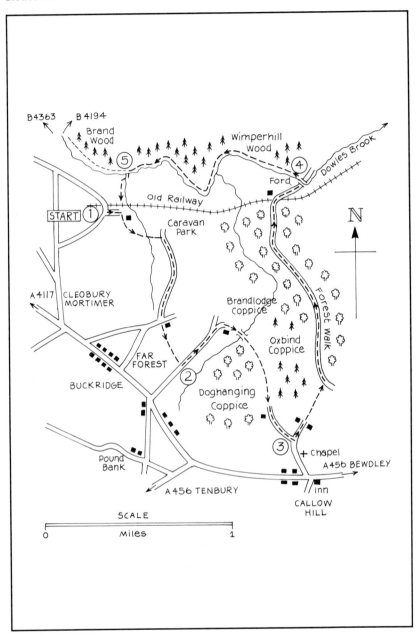

Route 26

Wyre Forest 5½ miles

Start

About halfway between Bewdley and Cleobury Mortimer on the A4117 is the village of Far Forest. Take the minor road north from Far Forest signposted Wyre Forest. After about half a mile turn right at Triangle Farm along a minor road. Continue to where a signposted bridleway dips to the right at a sharp left-hand bend. Park on the grass verge nearby. (OS Landranger Sheet 138, GR 727758).

Route

1. *Walk down the steep lane under the trees. At a left-hand bend, take the path to the right of a cottage called the Newells. Cross a stream and bear left to enter woodland. Climb a slope to reach a lane near the entrance to a caravan park. Turn right, and at a junction fork right along a minor road. In about half a mile, at a T-junction, cross a stile directly opposite and keep a hedge on the left across a field. Continue along a field to a stile and keep on to reach a lane.*

2. *Turn left and continue as far as a path on the right by a bungalow (Greenwood). Follow this path and keep on along the left side of a bungalow garden (Brantwood). Descend to cross a stream by a plank bridge. Enter woodland (Oxbind Coppice) and climb steadily to the top of the slope. Ignore side paths and keep straight on along a grassy track between fields, passing a farm on the right by a stile alongside a gate. Follow the lane to a T-junction.*

3. *Those wishing to visit the Royal Forester Inn should turn right here, cross a road and then turn to the left. To continue the walk turn left and follow the rough track through a farmyard and into a wood. Keep left at a bridleway sign (blue arrow) and follow these signs to meet a metalled forest track. Turn left along this and follow it for about a mile, passing Park House on the left, to cross a bridge with a ford to the right.*

4. *From the bridge, turn left along the bridleway, with a stream (Dowles Brook) on the left and conifer woodland on the right.*

5. *In about a mile when the track climbs and bends sharply to the right, bear left across the brook by the footbridge below. Cross another footbridge on the right and climb a path to join a lane. Pass a cottage, a dismantled railway bridge and The Newells and climb up to the road and your car.*

reminding us that forestry, like all other forms of land use, has an economic as well as a scenic value.

Refreshments
Callow Hill — The Royal Forester Inn: Lunches and snacks, family room, garden, children welcome.

Access by Bus
Far Forest is on the Birmingham-Kidderminster-Hereford route (Midland Red West).

Footbridge and ford, Dowles Brook, Wyre Forest

Speedwell Castle, Brewood (Route 32)

Severn Valley Railway

Arley and Severn Valley Railway

Outline
Arley Railway Station − Arley − River Severn − Highley Railway Station

Summary
This is a gentle walk alongside the banks of the serene Severn between two villages. They have seen their railway come and go but only to return triumphantly as a leisure route. The walk is enhanced by a nostalgic trip on the line and when you're walking you are bound to hear, smell and catch a glimpse of a passing train. It makes for a great family outing. Don't forget the picnic.

Attractions
You might well have seen Arley before, perhaps on television or at the cinema, for it is a very popular location with film makers. They are right to choose here for the entire line is soaked in nostalgia. There are usually several engines working the line; firemen stoking boilers, whistles blowing in the distance and smoke and steam in the air.

Both Arley and Highley stations have won awards for their authentic re-creation of rural Great Western stations depicting earlier decades. Trains run daily throughout the main season and most weekends during the winter months. Check with the Severn Valley Railway before travelling on (01299) 403816.

The ancient market centre of Bridgnorth is worth the detour. There is a direct pedestrian bridge from the railway station to the town centre, at one time a fortress settlement bounded by defensive walls. The Cliff Railway provides an easier option than walking up and down the steps between High and Low town. It is 100 years old and the steepest of its kind in Britain.

Refreshments
There are ample refreshments available at the railway or at one of the public houses in Arley and Highley.

Public Transport
The only way to travel to Arley is by the Severn Valley Railway!

Route 27

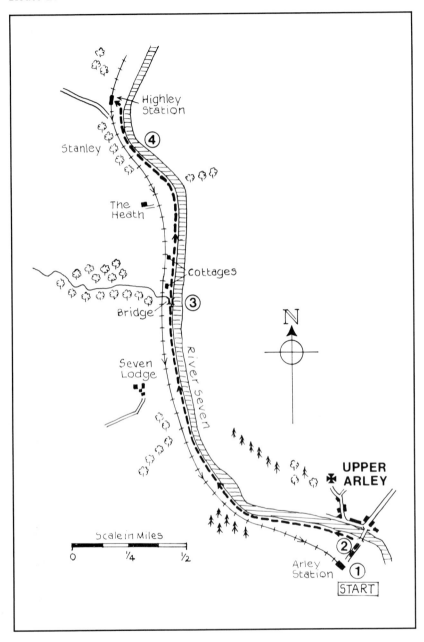

128

Route 27

Arley and the Severn Valley Railway

2½ miles

Start

Arley Railway Station, Severn Valley Railway (OS Landranger Sheet 138, GR 764799).

Route

1. *From Arley station turn left down the hill towards the village, which is for the most part on the opposite bank (across a pedestrian bridge) and well worth the detour. Otherwise, pass the Harbour Inn and follow the road around to the left to the old ferry point. Just before, the path proceeds ahead to a kissing gate which leads into fields.*

2. *Once through, keep ahead along a well worn path for the best part of the walk, through pockets of wood between lush riverside pastures where people while the day away fishing in quiet contemplation. The path continues along the river bank for the entire length of the journey, crossing five stiles (most of which are waymarked with a Severn Way marker) until you reach a footbridge over a tributary, the Borle Brook.*

3. *The path then continues more or less along the river bank for the next half mile or so, passing near to a few restored houses and cottages to be seen to your left.*

4. *You will soon catch sight of Highley station ahead and a few surrounding houses. Leave the riverside path to rise up to a gate and stile by a garden. Cross the stile and at the road bear right to the Ship Inn should refreshment be required. Then turn next left to climb the steps up to Highley Railway Station, as pretty as a picture on a late summer's day. You'll hear the train coming from miles away and there's a tense air just before its arrival, but then that's part of the excitement of a rural steam railway.*

Kinver

Kinver

Outline

The White Hart, Kinver − Jubilee Gardens − Hyde Bridge −
Whitting Horse Bridge − Kinver Church − Kinver

Summary

The walk offers an opportunity to walk through pastures to the Staffordshire and
Worcestershire Canal and then along its picturesque banks for a mile. The ramble then
climbs up to the impressive landmark of Kinver Church, which can be seen for miles
around. There's a final drop down to street level.

Attractions

Kinver is an ancient settlement which has numerous interesting historic buildings such
as the half-timbered Old Grammar School. Kinver Edge has been an attraction for
over a hundred years, but at the turn of the century its popularity was so great that
local entrepreneurs built the Kinver Light Railway through to Stourbridge which
remained in service until the 1930s.

Kinver Edge, a magnificent bluff above the village, is the site of an early camp
and in medieval times it became part of a hunting forest. During the last century
dwellings were hewn out of the red sandstone at Holy Austen rock. Several of them
have been restored and are open to the public now. The area is administered by the
National Trust.

The Staffordshire and Worcestershire Canal brought trade to the village during the
early decades of the 19th century. The navigation must be one of Brindley's finest
achievements, for it is a canal of great beauty and architectural merit. Kinver is now
a popular calling point for those cruising the canal down to Stourport or up to Great
Haywood.

Refreshments

Kinver has several cafes, restaurants and public houses, so there's plenty of choice
here.

Public Transport

There is a regular daily bus service from Stourbridge to Kinver.

Route 28

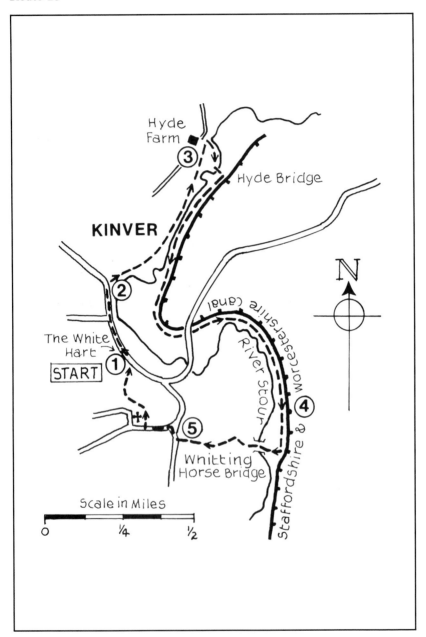

Hyde
Farm
③
Hyde Bridge

KINVER

②

The White
Hart
①
START

Staffordshire & Worcestershire Canal

River Stour

④

⑤

Whitting
Horse Bridge

N

Scale in Miles

0   ¼   ½

Route 28

Kinver

3 miles

Start

The White Hart, Kinver (OS Landranger Sheets 138 and 139, GR 845835).

Route

1. *Cross the main street from The White Hart and bear left. Follow the road past the Jubilee Gardens and go right by Mill House along the access road to the British Legion Club. On the right is the Kinver and West Midland Society of Model Engineers. To the right of the playground is the site of the old Light Railway.*

2. *The path runs to the right of the community centre and ahead through a playing field. Go through a kissing gate and proceed through pastures where horses graze. It continues along a corralled section to a farm where you walk between a stable and wall at Hyde Farm.*

3. *There is a good view back here to Kinver Church and the Edge. The path exits on to a road. Go right by the farm to cross the bridge over the river and then join the towpath where there is a wooden seat by Hyde Bridge and lock. Go right to walk along the towpath to the locks at Mill Lane. The Vine public house is on the left.*

4. *Follow the towpath under the road and then. as the canal curves right to Whitting Horse Bridge, leave the towpath to go right and pass by Bridge Cottage and the Anchor Hotel. Follow the road as it rises towards the village, but go through the kissing gate on the left. Head slightly right up the field to a corner, through a kissing gate and along a path which runs by a garden fence.*

5. *Exit on to the road and go right to drop down a little to a junction. Be careful here. Turn left and then go right up the drive to St Peter's Church. A track passes to the right of the church and descends through a gap in the wall. Take care on the path as it is steep in places. At the crossroads continue ahead. This leads to the High Street by The White Hart.*

Himley Hall

Baggeridge Country Park

Outline
Gospel End − Baggeridge Country Park − Himley Hall −
Woody Park − Gospel End

Summary
A gentle walk mainly through Baggeridge Country Park to the parklands of Himley
Hall. There's plenty of space for the children to run around, cascading waters and
pools and woodlands fit for hide and seek. Well marked paths and gentle rises only
on this ramble.

Attractions
Baggeridge Country Park, established next to the Baggeridge Brick Works, is a good
example of restoration of a landscape from previous workings. There is a visitor
centre and a number of short walks throughout the park.

The park leads down to Himley Hall, at one time the home of the Earls of Dudley.
Built in the 1820s by William Atkinson, the hall supersedes earlier buildings. Recent
restoration work will enable the hall to be developed into a museum depicting the great
works of glass-making for which the area is renowned.

The landscaped gardens are kept well and are a joy to walk at any time of the year,
but the children will almost certainly want to make a bee-line for the miniature railway
near to the lodge gate.

Refreshments
Light refreshment is available at Baggeridge Country Park and at Himley Hall. The
Summerhouse public house in Gospel End is very popular and there is a large garden
for children.

Public Transport
There is a bus service from Dudley to Gospel End.

Route 29

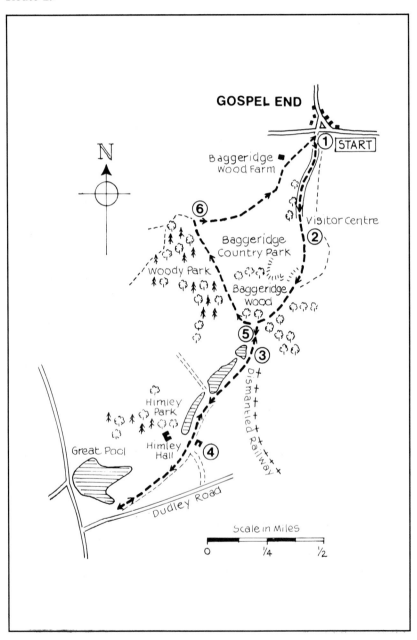

Route 29

Baggeridge Country Park   4 miles

Start

Gospel End – entrance to Baggeridge Country Park opposite the road to Penn Common (OS Landranger Sheet 139, GR 899937).

Route

1. *Walk into Baggeridge Country Park. Walk along the verge beside the narrow road which leads to the visitor centre. There are opportunities to cut the road corners through parkland.*

2. *Walk into the car park to the left of the visitor centre and through a grass amphitheatre. This leads to an aggregate path. Go right here and walk down to a junction. Bear left over a footbridge and you will see Spring and Island Pools to your right. There are little diversions to the water's edge, but do keep an eye on the kids!*

3. *Otherwise keep left at the turnings for both pools, continuing ahead by the stream (waymarked in red) to Island Pool. The path runs alongside the pool and crosses a stile on to a main track. Bear left and walk into Himley Park with Rock Pool beneath a wooded bluff on your right where you can see small carved caves. The track becomes a road and leads to the restored buildings of Himley Hall.*

4. *Go left and right to follow an avenue of trees to a lodge gate and a miniature railway. There are good views across to Great Pool, the largest of the lakes created here. Retrace your steps back into Baggeridge Country Park, rising by the pools to a point above Spring Pool.*

5. *Follow the red waymarked route left here down to the stream and over a footbridge. Rise up steps and cross a stile, then walk ahead through the aptly named Woody Park. The path becomes a track and runs through this quietest of spots.*

6. *It leaves the wood momentarily to meet a cross track. Go right here and walk up the bank into woodland again. The clear track and path runs up to the farm buildings of Baggeridge Wood Farm. Cross a stile and go right to join a small path which re-enters the woodland. This runs through to a track where you bear left and left again at the next junction for Gospel End. Those parked at Baggeridge Country Park should bear right instead.*

Leaving the Netherton Tunnel

Tipton

Outline
Tipton — Dudley Port — Netherton Tunnel — Wolverhampton Canal —
Dudley Canal Junction — Tipton

Summary
This walk follows the canals of the Black Country and is therefore level except for
occasional steps. The Main Line canal accommodates the Black Country Cycleway,
so look out for cyclists. Children love the idea of walking into the Netherton Tunnel,
so take a torch for it is dark within a short distance.

Attractions
The Black Country Musuem is a must to visit. It brings to life the heritage of the Black
Country and children will love the dozens of things they can do on site. There's a
replica coal mine, trams, and a reconstruction of a Black Country village. The boat
tours into the Dudley Tunnels bring more fun, as you may get a chance to leg the boat
through a section and in the dark!

Dudley is the capital of the Black Country and Dudley Zoo and Castle have been
attractions throughout the decades. Nearby Wrens Nest is also a good place for a
walk, especially if your family is interested in rock formations and fossils.

Tipton, where the walk begins, is a small shopping centre. The Fountain Inn in
the main street was home to the "Tipton Slasher", a boxer who trained here during
the 1850s. He was something of a celebrity in the Midlands, as for seven years he
retained his championship. There is a statue in Tipton which commemorates the
fighter.

The canals of the West Midlands provide green lungs for the urban conurbation.
This is as true of the Black Country as anywhere. There are several exceptional
features and the Netherton Tunnel is one of them. It was completed in the late 1850s
to provide more capacity through the Black Country than offered by the Dudley
Tunnel. At 3,027 yards it is long by any standards. The towpath used to be lit at one
time, firstly by gas lamps. There is no lighting now, so make sure the children have
torches if you are going to walk any length of it.

Refreshments
There are shops and inns in Tipton, including The Fountain, which has seats outside.

Public Transport
Tipton is well served by bus and train on a daily basis.

Route 30

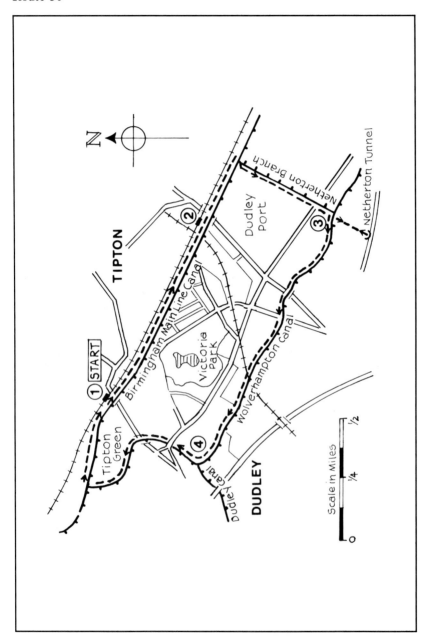

Route 30

Tipton   4½ miles

Start

At Tipton Railway Station, which is next to the canal (OS Landranger Sheet 139, GR 957926).

Route

1. *From Tipton station turn right to join the canal towpath on the left hand side of Owen Street. Continue ahead to walk along the towpath of the Birmingham Main Line canal. It is as straight as an arrow, but children are bemused by the busy railway line next door.*

2. *Pass Dudley Port railway station and soon afterwards you come to the junction with the Netherton Branch signposted to Hawne Basin. Go over the footbridge and continue along the towpath until the portals of the magnificent Netherton Tunnel. Be tempted to walk for a little in the dark to get the feeling of it.*

3. *Return to the overbridge and canal buildings. Go left to climb up to the Wolverhampton Canal. Go right here to walk along the towpath. This is the old canal and hence is more circuitous, following the contours and winding its way through modern housing designed to fit in with canal heritage.*

4. *Pass by the junction with the Dudley Canal and a route up to the Black Country Museum. Otherwise follow the Wolverhampton Canal back to the park in Tipton, where a statue of the Tipton Slasher stands. You can walk down to Factory Junction, where you cross to the Main Line towpath again. Bear right for Tipton Railway Station.*

Kingswood Common

Outline
Kingswood Common – Husphins Farm – Oaken – Oaken Lawn – Kingswood Common

Summary
An easy, level walk, which is on grassland but for a single field. In one field they grow fine turf and you may wish to change into carpet slippers. Twice you cross the railway, a main line so you might see any sort of train. After the second crossing the landscape is more wooded, and you can divert to look at the pretty village of Oaken. The walk back largely follows the long narrow common of Oaken Lawn, a delicious place with little woods and lawny green areas. Hilariously muddy.

Attractions
Kingswood Common and Oaken Lawn are both Commons. This means land that is owned by a particular person, who may now be a company or local council, but over which other people, but not the general public, have certain legal rights. So typically, a Common belonged to the Lord of the Manor, but through ancient custom the people of a nearby village might have rights to graze cattle, collect firewood or dig turf. Many Commons, including these two, are now owned by the District or Parish Councils who allow public access. There may also be public rights of way over Commons, as over any other land, in which case you can use them no matter what the owner says.

Kingswood Common is a modest, wooded triangle beside the A41. The trees are mainly oaks and birch with a shrub layer of hazel, brambles and gorse. On the wide, grassy lawn near the road are picnic tables. Parts of this popular family play and picnic place have been badly eroded by human feet and probably rabbits nibbling seedlings. These areas have been fenced off to encourage the spread of undergrowth.

Oaken Lawn is a narrow, thousand yard strip of grass and woodland which hides two cottages. In an ordered landscape of fields and hedges and carefully managed farms, it comes as an exciting and subversive burst of tangled, untidy, fertile, nature.

Park Farm near the start of the walk seems to be a chunky, handsome, sandstone house with a recent brick extension. However, as you pass you realise that it is really a brick house with sandstone facing. Even so, the stonework is so attractive that it is a pleasant trick.

Near the railway are a couple of huts used by the "Kinver Aeronauts Radio Control Society" who fly their model planes in the field.

Oaken is a charming little village of flowery gardens, though there are few old houses. The centrepiece is a brick terrace with attractive Georgian proportions, though both end houses seem to be recent extensions.

At three places along the walk are small, new plantations. Just after the second railway crossing is a field corner growing wild cherry, oak, beech, rowan, red oak, Scots pine and Norway spruce. In the second plantation are flowering shrubs with hazel, maple and beech, alder, cherry, red oak and rowan. Lastly, after the village is a roadside clump of young alder. All three areas are quite small, but they can be multiplied right across the Midlands to help restore some of our lost woodland.

Refreshments
The Foaming Jug is not on the walk, but by the A41 near Oaken. Kingswood Common and Oaken Lawn both have picnic tables.

Public Transport
Buses pass − details from the County Council on 01785 223344.

Kingswood Common

Route 31

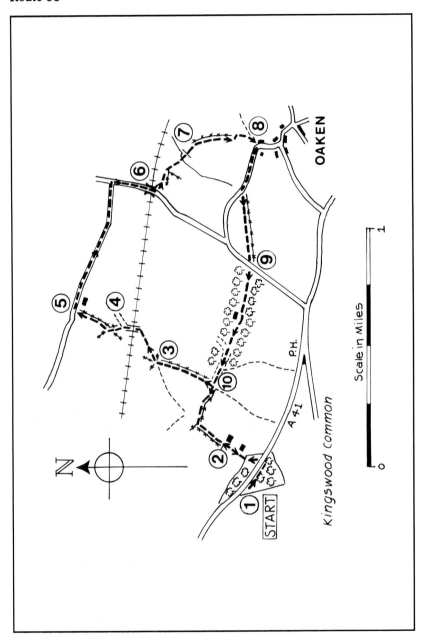

Route 31

Kingswood Common   **4 miles**

Start

A small, wooded area on the A41 north of Wolverhampton, map reference SJ 835029. Landranger map 127 – Stafford and Telford. Parking area.

Route

1. *In the car park, face the A41, then turn right and walk through the bushes, etc. Keep parallel with the road, but take the first path left to the A41. Cross and take the track into Park Farm (via a gate) to its end at a gate.*

2. *Cross the left corner stile. Walk with the hedge on your left and cross the next stile to a field. Turn right and through the gate. Follow the field edge track, pass the next gate, round the field corner, and go on about 200 yards to take a stile on the right.*

3. *Cross the field diagonally to about 30 yards right of the railway bridge and meet a track. Cross the bridge, and at the bottom of the slope take the first gate LEFT (not ahead).*

4. *Go to the far right field corner and cross the stile. Go right, cross the next stile, then walk with the hedge on your right to a stile and lane.*

5. *Go right about ½ mile to a T-junction. Go right to the railway bridge.*

6. *Cross the bridge, and at its end take the path left, down to a stile and field. Cross towards the far right corner and cross a stile. Follow the fenced path to a stile and field.*

7. *Walk with the fence on your left past two gates and via two stiles, then cross the field corner stile left into a plantation. Go through to the kissing gate and track. Go right via a stile and right bend to a lane. (Oaken is to the left. Go and have a look).*

8. *Go right about 400 yards (past the last house) to a right bend with three gates on the left. Cross the stile by the right hand gate. Walk with the hedge on your left and cross a stile to a lane.*

9. *Take the track opposite and keep the SAME STRAIGHT LINE for about ½ mile; - track continues to a sharp left bend, - take the path ahead through a small wood, - keep the same line along a narrow field to a house on the right, - follow the track to a cross ways, - take the earth track ahead and through the gate.*

10. *(Rejoins outward route). Follow the grass track through the next gate, then cross the stile left. Walk with the hedge on your right to the stile and track, which follow back to the A41 and start.*

Brewood and Chillington Hall

Outline
Coven Road − Giffard's Cross − Hunting Bridge − Brewood −
Giffard's Cross − Coven Road

Summary
An unusual figure of eight walk which twice meets the long, straight, tree lined Lower
Avenue which was once an approach to Chillington Hall. There are several pebbly,
sandy tracks which are a feature of this part of the world, and a good deal of
Shropshire Union Canal. You walk through Brewood, an uncommonly attractive
village. This is level, easy walking, but you meet a fair dollop of mud on the Avenue
and the canal towpath.

Attractions
Lower and Upper Avenue were built as grand carriage drives to Chillington Hall,
home of the Giffard family since the 12th century. The present hall is 18th century
and the surrounding parkland was landscaped by Capability Brown.

Between Upper and Lower Avenue is Giffard's Cross, where in 1513 Sir John
Giffard saw a panther (repeat − panther) menacing a poor woman and her child.
From the house he shot the springing beast with a bolt from his crossbow. The
incident gave rise to the Giffard motto − "Prenez haleine, tirez forte" − meaning
"take breath, pull hard", which is what Sir John's son is supposed to have said as
he came up behind his aiming father. Given this silly interruption, the poor woman
was jolly lucky. So was Sir John, because we are not certain that modern rifles are
accurate at nearly 2,000 yards.

You will probably be disappointed because panthers are rarely seen at Chillington.
The late menacing one turns out to have been an escaped present from an Oriental
friend.

Chillington Hall was built in 1724 and extended in 1786/89. A grand red brick
country house, it has stone quoins and dressings, stately Ionic columns and imposing
balustraded parapets. Go and have a look. The opening times are shown on a notice
board near the entrance.

The two Avenues together are 2 miles long and lined by stout oaks and beech. Only
Lower Avenue is open to the public by virtue of a right of way. It has been virtually
abandoned as part of the estate and is now a twilight of self-seeded holly, brambles,
oaks and beech. There are a few hornbeam in the north-west corner. At about half
way are the balustraded parapets of Avenue Bridge which carries the drive over the
Shropshire Union Canal. It was designed and built by Telford in 1826, a fine example
of the expensive gestures which had to be made to powerful landowners to secure a
canal's Act of Parliament.

Much of this walk follows the Shropshire Union Canal, which was completed in

1835. This was a second generation canal. The first group were built in the later 1700s. Limited experience, technology and finance available to the early engineers, such as Brindley, Jessop and Outram, led them to avoid the expense and difficulty of cuttings and embankments, so they built canals which changed level as little as possible, dreaming around the contours, looping and wandering through the landscape.

By the 1820s these aqueous meanders had become an expensive and time-wasting nuisance. The second generation canals used greater investment and improved methods to build vast earthworks. So Telford drove the SU on a near straight line from Autherley Junction north of Wolverhampton, through the gentle Shropshire countryside to Nantwich in Cheshire. But the SU is no less beautiful than the meandering older canals. Perhaps its directness lends it a tinge of purposeful excitement − going somewhere.

The first part of the canal walk is just below field level, then comes a long cutting between high banks of hawthorn, elder, nettles and brambles. Finally, near Brewood the canal strides over a high embankment. The SU has some of the most beautiful bridges on the system, broad and mellow sandstone arches. They have attractive names. In turn you meet Hunting Bridge, Park Bridge, Chillington Bridge, Avenue Bridge, Giffard's Cross Bridge, Deans Hall Bridge, School Bridge and Brewood Bridge.

Brewood (pronounced Brood) comes into view from the high canal embankment, seen over meadows with the spire of the church of St Mary & St Chad lofting over the skyline. This is a delightful little town, or large village. There are several nice Georgian houses, but most of the town is Victorian or quite recent. The church has a 13th century chancel and the north aisle has medieval windows, but there has been a lot of Victorian restoration. In the chancel are four whacking great recumbent alabaster figures of bearded Giffards and their wives. Quite dotty is Speedwell Castle in the Market Place, which was built (for some reason) in 1750. Although basically a three storied house, it has battlements and large bays with a mixture of round arched and ogee headed windows. It was paid for by Speedwell, the Duke of Bolton's racehorse.

Refreshments
Pubs and teashops in Brewood.

Public Transport
Buses pass − details from the County Council on 01785 223344.

Route 32

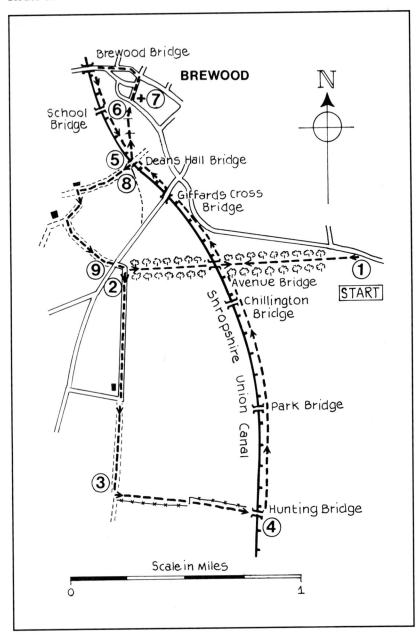

148

Route 32

Brewood and Chillington Hall $\qquad$ 6¾ miles

Start

Park on the wide verge by the gates to the Avenue on the road between Brewood and Coven, north-west of Wolverhampton. (Take care not to obstruct the field entrance). Map reference SJ 899076, OS Landranger Map 127 – Stafford and Telford.

Route

1. *Take the small gate on the left side of the stone entrance. Follow the Avenue for just over 1 mile to a lane.*

2. *Walk left about ½ mile to a house right (The Gables) and a right bend. Take the track ahead (via a gate) for about ⅓ mile to the overhead power lines. Continue for 100 yards and take the gateway left just before the hedge.*

3. *Walk with the hedge on your right (past a gateway right) to the field corner, and take a gate right. Go immediately left into the next field and resume your previous direction (with the hedge on your left) to a gate in the field corner. Take the gate and cross the bridge. Turn right through another gate, then immediately right over a stile to the towpath.*

4. *Go under the bridge and follow the canal for nearly 2 miles: - 1st section just below field level (½ mile) - 2nd section in a deep cutting (about 1¼ miles) ending at Bridge 13 and the start of the embankment with Brewood Church in view.*

5. *Take the stile right down to the field. Bear left to cross a low brick bridge, cross a stile, then walk with the fence/hedge on your right (via a stile) to a stile and track. Go left a few paces and take the walled path right to the village.*

6. *Go leftwards round the church, following the main road up the main street to the crossroads facing The Lion.*

7. *Go left (Bishop's Wood road) for about 350 yards to the bridge and join the canal. DON'T GO UNDER THE BRIDGE. Follow the towpath for nearly ½ mile under the first bridge to the next (No 13 again). Take the steps up to the track.*

8. *Go right, at the junction go left, to a crossroads of tracks. Take the pebbly track left to the road.*

9. *Take the lane opposite and round the right bend to enter the end of the Avenue again, left. Follow the Avenue back to the start.*

Gifford Cross, Brewood

Working narrowboat on the Shropshire Union Canal

Avenue Bridge

USEFUL INFORMATION

PUBLIC TRANSPORT: Warwickshire and the West Midlands:
British Rail: Telephone 0121 643 2711
Bus information: Centro Hotline: 0121 200 2700
  West Midlands Travel: 0121 236 8313
  Midland Red North: 01827 63861
  Midland Red West: 0121 200 2700
   01905 359393

TOURIST INFORMATION CENTRES

Birmingham: BCVP Ticket Shop and Information Office, City Arcade. 0121 643 2514.
National Exhibition Centre: 0121 780 4321.
Central Library: 0121 235 4651.
Birmingham Airport: Information Desk. 0121 767 7145/6.
Birmingham International Convention Centre: 0121 665 6116.
Bromsgrove: 49 Worcester Road. 01527 31809.
Coventry: Bayley Lane. 01203 832303.
Droitwich Spa Heritage Centre: Heritage Way. 01905 774312.
Kenilworth: The Library, 11 Smalley Place. 01926 52595/50708.
Leamington Spa: The Jephson Lodge, Jephson Gardens, The Parade. 01926 311470.
Nuneaton: The Library, Church Street. 01203 384027.
Rugby: The Library, St Matthew Street. 01788 535348.
Solihull: Central Library, Homer Road. 0121 704 6130. Stratford-upon-Avon: Bridgefoot.
01789 293127/294466.
Warwick: The Court House, Jury Street. 01926 492212.
Worcester: Guildhall, High Street. 01905 723471, ext 202.

WET WEATHER ALTERNATIVES—

completely or partly under cover (admission free where stated).

It is advisable to check times of opening. For attractions in Birmingham and Coventry refer to local Tourist Information Centres.

MUSEUMS, GALLERIES AND CRAFT WORKSHOPS

Abbey Barn, Abbey Fields, Kenilworth. Norman stonework from Abbey ruins, tiles, gargoyles, farm and tannery tools, local finds. Admission free. Tel: 01926 53574.

Albany Fine China Museum, 42 Lowesmoor, Worcester. Tel: 01905 726320.

Antique Doll Collection, Golden Cross Inn, Wixford Road, Ardens Grafton, near Bidford-on-Avon. Admission free. Tel: 01789 772420.

Avoncroft Museum of Buildings, Stoke Heath, near Bromsgrove. Open March-November.

Berkswell Museum, Berkswell village. Local memorabilia, implements, etc. Tel: 01676 33322/32371/33678.

Bewdley Museum, The Shambles, Load Street. Open March-November.

Birmingham Museum and Art Gallery, Chamberlain Square, Birmingham. Tel: 0121 235 2834.

Birmingham Railway Museum, 670 Warwick Road, Tyseley, Birmingham. Open April-September. Tel: 0121 707 4696.

Black Country Museum, Tipton Road, Dudley. Tel: 0121 557 9643.

Bromsgrove Museum, 26 Birmingham Road, Bromsgrove. Also Craft Centre. Open all year.

The Commandery, Civil War Centre, Sidbury, Worcester. Open all year.

Droitwich Heritage Centre, Heritage Way, Droitwich. Open all year.

Edgehill Battle Museum, The Estate Yard, Farnborough Hall, near Banbury. Armour, costumes, etc, of Battle of Edgehill, 1642. Tel: 01295 89593 or 01296 332213.

Forge Mill National Needle Museum, Needle Mill Lane, Redditch. Open all year.

Hatton Craft Centre, Hatton. Craft workshops in converted farm buildings. Rare breeds park. Shops, cafe. Open daily.

The Herbert Art Gallery and Museum, Jordan Well, Coventry. Admission free. Tel: 01203 832381.

James Gilbert Rugby Football Museum, St Matthew's Street, Rugby. Rugby memorabilia, shop where balls made since 1842. Admission free. Tel: 01788 536500.

The Jinney Ring Craft Centre, Hanbury, near Bromsgrove. Limited opening Easter-Christmas.

Leamington Spa Art Gallery and Museum, Avenue Road. Paintings, pottery and local history. Admission free. Tel: 01926 426559.

Manor Farm Craft Centre, Wood Lane, Earlswood. Craft workshop, farm shop, home-made ice cream, tea room. Admission free. Tel: 01564 62729.

Middleton Hall Craft Centre, near Tamworth. Working craftsmen and women. Admission free.

Midland Air Museum, Coventry Airport, Baginton. Over 20 historic aircraft. Sir Frank Whittle Jet Heritage Centre. Tel: 01203 301033.

Midland Bus and Transport Museum, Chapel Lane, Wythall. Open weekends and Bank Holidays, April-November.

Museum of British Road Transport, Hales Street, Coventry. Tel: 01203 832425.

Museum of Country Bygones, Louisa Ward Close, off High Street, Marton, near Leamington Spa. Craftsmen's tools, household and dairy equipment and wagons.

Museum of Science and Industry, Newhall Street, Birmingham. Open Monday to Friday, Sundays. Admission free. Tel: 0121 235 1661.

National Motorcycle Museum, on A45 at Bickenhill. 600 British machines from 1898 onwards. Tel: 01675 53311.

Nuneaton Library, Church Street. Local history collection and George Eliot photographs, letters, books, etc. Admission free. Tel: 01203 384027/347006.

Nuneaton Museum and Art Gallery, Riversley Park. Local history, archaeology, art and the George Eliot collection. Admission free. Tel: 01203 350595.

Oldwych Gallery, Oldwych House Farm, Fen End, Kenilworth. Paintings by Midlands artists. Admission free. Tel: 01676 33552.

Rugby Library and Exhibition Gallery, St Matthew's Street. Loan exhibitions and local artists. Admission free.

St John's House, Coten End, Warwick. Branch of county museum and Royal Warwickshire Regiment Museum. Admission free. Tel: 01926 410410, ext 2021.

Severn Valley Railway, Railway Station, Bewdley: Tel: 01299 403866.

Teddy Bear Museum, 19 Greenhill Street, Stratford-upon-Avon. Hundreds of teddies in Elizabethan setting.

Toy Museum, Whitefriars Gate, Coventry. Tel: 01203 227560.

Tudor House Museum, Friar Street, Worcester. Open all year.

Warwickshire Museum, Market Place, Warwick. County museum. History, geology, Sheldon's great tapestry map, etc. Admission free. Tel: 01926 410410, ext 2500.

Warwickshire Yeomanry Museum, The Court House, Jury Street, Warwick. Uniforms, arms, swords, etc. See also The Court House below. Admission free. Tel: 01926 492212.

Wellesbourne Watermill, Mill Farm, Wellesbourne, near Stratford-upon-Avon. Waterwheel, machinery, video, teas.

Wellesbourne Wartime Museum. Former Wellesbourne Mountford RAF station. World War II relics, in underground bunker. Battle operations control room. Admission free.

Worcester City Museum and Art Gallery, Foregate Street, Worcester. Open all year. Tel: 01905 25371.

Worcestershire County Museum, Hartlebury Castle, near Kidderminster. Open March-November.

Worcester Royal Porcelain and Dyson Perrins Museum. Open all year.

CASTLES, HOUSES AND CHURCHES

Anne Hathaway's Cottage, Shottery, near Stratford-upon-Avon. Thatched farmhouse, home of Shakespeare's wife. Tel: 01789 292100.

Arbury Hall, near Nuneaton. Unique example of Gothic Revival architecture. Tel: 01203 382804.

Baddesley Clinton Hall, near Lapworth: National Trust. Moated medieval manor house. Open March-October (Wednesday-Sunday). Tel: 01564 783294.

Bordesley Abbey, Redditch. Ruins. Open all year.

Charlecote Park, near Stratford-upon-Avon. National Trust. Elizabethan. Tudor gatehouse, deer park. Tel: 01789 470277.

Chester House, Knowle Library, 1667-9 High Street, Knowle. Elizabethan town house, with parts from 1400. Admission free. Tel: 01564 775840.

Collegiate Church of St Mary, Old Square, Warwick. 15th century Beauchamp Chapel, Norman crypt. Admission free. Tel: 01926 400771.

Coughton Court, near Alcester. National Trust. Mainly Elizabethan. Gunpowder Plot connection. Tel: 01789 762435.

The Court House, Jury Street, Warwick. 18th century Italian style, including Mayor's Parlour and Ballroom. Also Warwickshire Yeomanry Museum see above. Admission free. Tel: 01926 492212.

Coventry Cathedral, Priory Street, Coventry. Tel: 01203 227597.

Farnborough Hall, near Banbury. National Trust. Classical 18th century.

Greyfriars, Friar Street, Worcester. National Trust. Limited opening April-October.

Guildhall, Worcester. Open all year, Monday-Friday.

Hagley Hall, Hagley, near Stourbridge. Palladian house. Tel: 01592 882408.

Hall's Croft, Old Town, Stratford-upon-Avon. Tudor town house, home of Shakespeare's daughter and doctor son-in-law. Tel: 01789 292107.

Hanbury Hall, near Droitwich: National Trust. William and Mary style red brick house dated 1701. Open April-October. Tel: 01527 821214.

Harvard House, High Street, Stratford-upon-Avon. Rebuilt 1596. Early home of Katherine Rogers, mother of John Harvard (founder of Harvard University, USA). Tel: 01789 204507.

Harvington Hall, near Kidderminster. Open April-November.

Hawford Dovecote, 3 miles north of Worcester off A449. National Trust.

Holy Trinity Church, Old Town, Stratford-upon-Avon. Lovely riverside setting. Graves of William Shakespeare and Anne Hathaway. Admission free, but charge to view Shakespeare's grave. Tel: 01789 266316.

Kenilworth Castle, Kenilworth. 12th century. Open daily.

Lord Leycester Hospital, High Street, Warwick. Old soldiers' home since 1571. Chapel. Great Hall and Guildhall. Tel: 01926 491422.

Lunt Roman Fort, Baginton, near Coventry. Britain's only reconstructed Roman Fort. Tel: 01203 832381.

New Place/Nash's House, Chapel Street, Stratford-on-Avon. Foundations of Shakespeare's last home in Elizabethan garden. Period furniture and museum of Stratford's history. Tel: 01789 292325.

Packwood House, near Lapworth. National Trust. Timber-framed Tudor house. Famous yew garden. Open April-October (Wednesday-Sunday). Tel: 01564 782024.

Ragley Hall, near Alcester. 17th century Palladian. Tel: 01789 762090.

Sarehole Mill, Cole Bank Road, Hall Green, Birmingham. Working windmill. Open March-October. Admission free. Tel: 0121 777 6612.

Shakespeare's Birthplace, Henley Street, Stratford-upon-Avon. Half-timbered, with many original features. Shakespearean books, manuscripts, etc. Tel: 01789 204016.

Shakespeare's Countryside Museum and Mary Arden's House, Wilmcote, near Stratford-upon-Avon. Tudor farmstead. Museum of rural life and home of Shakespeare's mother. Tel: 01789 293455.

St. Mary's Guildhall, Bayley Lane, Coventry. Fine medieval guildhall. Open May-September. Tel: 01203 832381.

Tamworth Castle and Museum. Norman keep, Tudor chapel, Jacobean state apartments. Locally minted Saxon coin collection. Tel: 01827 63563.

Upton House, Edgehill. National Trust. Late 17th century. Outstanding collection of paintings. Tel: 01295 87266.

Warwick Castle. England's finest medieval castle. Many rooms, including Great Hall and Dungeon. Madame Tussaud tableau of "A Royal Weekend Party − 1898". Tel: 01926 495421.

Warwick Doll Museum, Oken's House. Collection of antique dolls, dolls' houses, toys, etc. Tel: 01926 495546 or 410410, ext 2500.

Wichenford Dovecote, 5½ miles NW of Worcester off B4204. National Trust.

OTHER PLACES OF INTEREST
Ashorne Hall Nickelodeon, Ashorne Hill, near Warwick. Collection of mechanical musical instruments. Live show on Sundays. Tel: 01926 651444.

Berkswell Windmill, Windmill Lane, Balsall Common. Tower mill, with original machinery (not working). Tel: 01676 33403.

Bosworth Battlefield and Visitor Centre, Market Bosworth. Tel: 01455 292239.

Cadbury World, Linden Road, Bournville, Birmingham. The ultimate chocolate experience! Tel: 0121 451 4180.

Clacks Farm, Boreley, Ombersley, Worcester. Open selected weekends, Spring-Autumn.

Clent Hills Country Park, near Birmingham.

Coombe Abbey Country Park, Brinklow Road, Binley, near Coventry. Visitor centre. Open every day April-September.

Drayton Manor Park, Fazeley, near Tamworth. House, gardens, amusement park, zoo. Tel: 01827 260260.

Jardinerie, Kenilworth Road, Hampton-in-Arden. Garden centre, aquatic centre and coffee shop. Admission free. Tel: 01675 52866.

Napton Windmill, Napton-on-the-Hill, near Southam.

Notcutts Garden Centre. Large covered sales area, children's playground, licensed restaurant. Admission free. Tel: 0121 744 4501.

Ryton Organic Gardens, Ryton-on-Dunsmore, Coventry. Rare breeds, shop, play area. Open every day. Tel: 01203 305517.

Severn Valley Railway (Holdings) plc, The Railway Station, Bewdley, Worcs. Tel: 01299 403816.

Spetchley Park, near Worcester. Open April-September.

Splashland, Tudor Grange Swimming Centre, Blossomfield Road, Solihull. High speed waterslide, bobsled run, children's area. Tel: 0121 704 5206.

Stratford Brass Rubbing Centre, Summerhouse, Royal Shakespeare Theatre, Avonbank Gardens. Unique collection of brass rubbing. Admission free. Tel: 01789 297671.

Stratford-upon-Avon Butterfly Farm, Tramway Walk. Europe's largest live butterfly safari. Tel: 01789 299288.

Twycross Zoo, Twycross, east of Tamworth. Finest primate collection in the country (the Brooke Bond chimps), etc. Tel: 01827 880250.

Tysoe Windmill, Tysoe, south-west of Edgehill.

Waseley Hills Country Park, near Bromsgrove.

West Midland Safari and Leisure Park, Spring Grove, Bewdley. Tel: 01299 402114.

Worcester Woods Country Park, near Worcester.

Wyre Forest Visitor Centre, near Bewdley. Open all year.

BIBLIOGRAPHY

Just a selection of useful publications, past and present:

Guide to English Heritage Properties – English Heritage.

The National Trust Handbook – The National Trust.

Places to Visit in the Heart of England – The Heart of England Tourist Board.

History, People and Places in Warwickshire – –Harold Parsons, 1975.

Warwickshire – Vivian Bird, 1973.

A Short History of Warwickshire and Birmingham – Vivian Bird, 1977.

Warwickshire: Shakespeare's County – Arthur Mee, 1936 (re-published 1991).

The Buildings of England – *Warwickshire* – Nikolaus Pevsner.

In the Forest of Arden – John Burman, 1948.

Rambles Round the Edge Hills and in the Vale of the Red Horse – George Miller, 1896 (re-published 1967).

The Centenary Way – Warwickshire County Council (11 leaflets).

Sutton Park – Its History and Wildlife – Douglas V Jones.

Warwick Castle – Official Guide.

Walking around Stoneleigh in Arden – Audrey V Gilbert, 1991.

Birmingham and Fazeley Canal – Birmingham Canal Walkway Guides, No 1: Gas Street Basin to Aston Junction.

Digbeth Canal – As above, No 3: Aston Junction to Warwick Bar.

Nicholson's Guide to the Waterways – *5: Midlands* – Robert Nicholson Publications.

From small beginnings, Scarthin Books has built up an extensive list of walking and local history books

PAPERBACKS

Our Village. Alison Uttley's Cromford. Alison Uttley. *Cromford, well-known as the site of the world's first water-powered cotton mill, is also fortunate to have as its chronicler the celebrated essayist and children's writer. Alison Uttley. This collection of essays vividly recalls scenes from the self-sufficient late Victorian village of her childhood. Illustrated by C.F. Tunnicliffe.* 72pp. ISBN 0 907758 08 8.

The Crich Tales. Unexpected Echoes from a Derbyshire Village. Geoffrey Dawes. *Tales of earthy humour and rural shrewdness, told in a village pub. Illustrations by Geoff Taylor.* 96pp. ISBN 0 907758 06 1.

Hanged for a Sheep. Crime in Bygone Derbyshire. E.G. Power. *A factual and entertaining survey of crime and the fight against it from 1750 to 1850.* 80pp. ISBN 0 907758 00 2.

The Cromford Guide. Freda Bayles and Janet Ede. *At last — a long-awaited, concise and comprehensive guide to this historic village. Based on three walks around the village and the surrounding countryside, The Cromford Guide points out the many features of interest past and present in this lively village.* 48pp. 5 maps + photographs. ISBN 0 907758 76 2.

St John's Chapel, Belper. The Life of a Church and a Community. E.G. Power. *The history of "The Foresters' Chapel" and the people it served, from the 13th century to the present. This book is not a guidebook for the antiquarian, but easy reading for anyone interested in the past life of Belper and the place of St John's Chapel in that life.* 40pp. ISBN 0 907758 11 8.

Pauper's Venture: Children's Fortune. The Lead Mines and Miners of Brassington. *A study of the lead mining community of Brassington. With gazetteer of sites.* 52pp. ISBN 0 907758 18 5.

Ancient Wells and Springs of Derbyshire. Peter J. Naylor. *The only book on the natural waters of Derbyshire.* 80pp. ISBN 0 907758 01 0.

Salad Days in Sutton. Charles W. Sanderson. *Childhood and youth in Sutton-in-Ashfield between the Wars. Contemporary photographs and drawings by the author.* 66pp. ISBN 0 907758 14 2.

Pipe Organs in Churches and Chapels of the Derwent and Ecclesbourne Valleys. Rodney Tomkins. *An absorbing guide to some 85 pipe organs in the area from Darley Abbey to Darley Dale.* 112pp. Photographs. ISBN 0 907758 88 6.

Driving the Clay Cross Tunnel. Cliff Williams. *An account of the (not inconsiderable) feat of driving a tunnel under Clay Cross for the Derby to Leeds railway in the 1830s.* 88pp. Photographs. ISBN 0 907758 07 X.

The Story of Holbrook. Doris Howe. *The history of Holbrook from the earliest settlement to the present day.* 84pp. Map and photographs. ISBN 0 907758 05 3.

HARDBACKS

Walls Across the Valley. The Building of the Howden and Derwent Dams. Brian Robinson. *An illustrated history of the work of the Derwent Valley Water Board, produced in collaboration with Severn Trent Water. Contains a wealth of previously unpublished photographs and diagrams, also 20 colour photographs. Of particular interest to students of social, railway and engineering history.* 256pp. Appendices, bibliography, index, duotone and colour illustrations. ISBN 0 907758 57 6.

Transformation of a Valley. Brian Cooper and Neville Cooper. *The lively and scholarly story of the Derwent Valley during the development of mines, mills and other industries. The most readable and authoritative guide to the industrial history of the area.* 316pp. With maps and 130 photographs of historic sites. Bibliography, index. ISBN 0 907758 17 7.

Derbyshire i' the Civil War. Brian Stone. *The only single-volume work on the subject. It traces the fighting : Derbyshire and the deeds of Derbyshire men elsewhere, and also looks at the plight of non-combatants and the personal animosities motivating leaders on both sides.* 157pp. Illustrated, with notes, bibliography and index. ISBN 0 907758 58 4.

Robert Bakewell: Artist Blacksmith. S. Dunkerley. *Thirty-two pages of colour photographs with opposing pages of commentary form the core of this unique life of the great 18th century craftsman in wrought iron.* 112pp. Bound in high-quality cloth. With line drawings, gazetteer and index. Limited to 750 signed copies. ISBN 0 907758 24 X.

HISTORICAL MONOGRAPHS

Waterways to Derby. A study of the Derwent Navigation and Derby Canal. Celia M. Swainson. *The battle to link Derby to the arteries of trade during the Industrial Revolution.* 64 pp. ISBN 0 907758 59 2.

Historic Farmhouses around Derby. Barbara Hutton. *A detailed study of the old brick and timber farmhouses of South Derbyshire and the Trent Valley.* 64pp. Full gazetteer/index. ISBN 0 907758 48 7.

Millclose: the Mine that Drowned. Lynn Willies, Keith Gregory, Harry Parker. *The story of Britain's largest-ever lead mine and the men who worked it.* 64pp. 59 illustrations. ISBN 0 907758 28 2.

LARGE FORMAT PAPERBACKS

The Seven Blunders of the Peak. A fresh look at some Derbyshire legends. Edited by Brian Robinson. *Derbyshire is rich in history and legend, not all based on fact. Seven well-known Derbyshire writers and historians put the record straight. Did Dorothy Vernon wade across the Wye? Was the Eyam plague the mumps? Is Little John really buried at Hathersage?* 128pp. Maps, tables and photographs. ISBN 0 907758 77 0.

The Clay Cross Calamities. Terry Judge. *Written by a miner turned historian, this book charts a 20-year period in the life of the Clay Cross coalmines, when it was a race between disaster and safer working conditions.* 112pp. Maps, diagrams and photographs. ISBN 0 907758 78 9.

With Courage & Trust. 20 years with police dogs. David Brown. *A serving policeman, David Brown describes the story of British police dogs, his own often hilarious experiences and shares many tips on training and care.* 128pp. Photographs. ISBN 0 907758 78 9.

THE FAMILY WALKS SERIES

The publishers welcome suggestions for future titles and will be pleased to consider manuscripts relating to Derbyshire from new and established authors.

Scarthin Books of Cromford, in the Peak District, are also leading new, second-hand and antiquarian booksellers, and are eager to purchase specialised material, both ancient and modern.

Contact Dr. D.J. Mitchell 01629 823272.